Journey to the Future:

A Roadmap for Success for Youth

Consuelo Castillo Kickbusch,

Lieutenant Colonel, U.S. Army [Retired]

IP Liberty Publishing Group
Durham, NC, USA

This publication is designed to provide accurate and authoritative information in regard to the subject matter covered. It is sold with the understanding that the publisher is not engaged in rendering legal, accounting or other professional service. From a Declaration of Principles jointly adopted by a Committee of the American Bar Association and a Committee of Publishers.

Publisher's Cataloging-in-Publication Data

Kickbusch, Consuelo Castillo
Journey to the Future: A roadmap for success for youth / Consuelo Castillo Kickbusch.
p. cm.

ISBN 1-893095-22-3 / 978-1-893095-22-9

Library of Congress Control Number: 2003111720

10 9 8 7 6 5 4 3 2 1

Dedication

First, I dedicate this book to the daughter I failed to understand. I tried, but life gave us those experiences we didn't expect which will eternally create great pain and sadness.

I chose to raise her and her siblings with boundaries. To me love has conditions. It's not easy to admit to yourself and others that while I have helped thousands of kids to think positively and change their lives for the better, this is one child I feel I failed to connect with.

She is doing fine and doing what she feels is best. I have missed her every day. I decided to give her the opportunity to live with her new family without much interference from me. I will always wonder if I made the right decision. My goal is to be there whenever she calls me or needs me.

Alicia, I am still your mom and will always love you. The family you once lived with misses you dearly. Congratulations upon your high school graduation and your four-year scholarship to college. I love your spirit and I feel deeply in my heart that you will always be what I affectionately call my "Tender Heart." Make your own history and be a leader. I am very proud of you.

Love always,
Your mom

Table of Contents

*Declaration of Independence (excerpt) • Patrick Henry's
Famous "Give Me Liberty" Speech March of 1775
(excerpt) • Lincoln's Gettysburg Address • President
Franklin Delano Roosevelt's "Human Freedom" Speech
(excerpt) • President Woodrow Wilson's "Genesis of Amer-
ica" Speech (excerpt) • President John F. Kennedy's 1961
Inaugural Address (excerpt) • Dr. Martin Luther King, Jr.'s
"I Have a Dream" Speech (excerpt)*

Acknowledgments

How do you say thank you to the thousands of children who graciously listened to my message. What's important to know is that they were the first inspiration for this book. *Thank you for reminding me school after school that I needed to write my thoughts to be shared with generations to come.*

I want to thank my husband, David and my children—Kenitha Calisa, Alicia Carmelina, Consuelo Panthel and the twins Delilah and Dolores—for their incredible support and encouragement. To my brothers and sisters and to my first leaders—my parents, thank you for always loving me. Thanks to Dr. Nora Comstock and Dr. Consuelo Ramirez who bravely got me started.

My most sincere thanks to Yolanda Uranga who helped me start the book and Pat Medina who even at the last minute was willing to edit and finish my last words, thank you from the bottom of my heart.

To Bil and Cher Holton, our publishing champions, thank you for taking the trip back to my barrio and helping me make this dream come true. I am so grateful to have met one of the most talented Latino artists, Ernesto Cuevas who graciously agreed to design the cover for my book. My most sincere thank-you to Matthew Russell for being an angel investor and purchasing the first copies of my book.

To all the teachers, administrators and staff who work daily in our children's lives and who in my opinion are the silent heroes of our country, thank you for inviting me to your schools. Who would have ever imagined that together we would touch the lives of 1 million children? To the U.S. Army, thank you for shaping my life and teaching me to be a leader.

Muchas Gracias, thank-you and many blessings.

Journey to the Future

Note to the Reader From the Publishers

It was our great pleasure—and privilege—in June of 2003 to accompany the author on a trip from San Antonio to her childhood barrio in Laredo, Texas. The purpose of the trip was for us to get a first-hand experience of the kind of environment the author came from as a small Mexican-American girl growing up in a border town.

Although there have been some modest improvements, the "Devil's Den," as it was called during the author's childhood, is pretty much in the same socio-economic condition as it was 25 years ago. As we toured the area with the author and her staff, we became thoroughly impressed with her passion for her work, her tremendous drive and determination to save the young people in America, and her respect and reverence for her heritage.

At one point on our tour, we paid an impromptu visit to an alcohol and drug abuse rehab center situated near the "last street in America." We watched in awe as the author ministered to the young men assigned there—and ministered is the appropriate word. The author spoke to those young people as Mother Teresa would have spoken to them—and that is not an exaggeration.

In all our years of publishing, we have not been touched as deeply by any other author. We witnessed her extraordinary ability to connect—psychologically, emotionally and spiritually—with young men whom society would just as soon throw away. We have no doubt she changed their lives that day—we were there, we saw how she mesmerized both the young people and the counselors.

If Consuelo Castillo Kickbusch is any indication of the type of lantern-hearted soul who can come from an impoverished barrio—then America still has a chance to tap the richness of its diversity and live up to its founding principles.

America is fortunate, indeed, to have produced a human being of Consuelo's caliber. The children of America are lucky to have her, too. And we feel privileged to publish this extraordinary book, which is a literary extension of her real-life ministry to the school children across America.

~ Bil & Cher Holton, {Publishers)

Why This Book?

- A Mother's Dying Wish -

My life was as good as it got for a woman in her early forties with a successful career, wonderful family, great kids, super husband, nice home, and a bright future. So why change my life so drastically? The time for this drastic change came in November 1995. The words were as clear then as they were when my mother spoke them to me in 1987. My life's work is the result of a mother's dying wish. It happened like this:

It was late November in 1987, and I was mid way through my master's degree program at San Jose State University in San Jose, California. I was studying Cybernetics, a discipline based on the interaction of man and machine. I

was focusing on the discipline of how systems and systems thinking are applied in our everyday lives. I was preparing myself to serve in the U. S. Army as a systems scientist. They paid for my education because they believed I had the potential to succeed in the U. S. Army as a career officer.

I loved the Army, to tell you the truth. It had afforded me the American dream of becoming successful in spite of my so-called disadvantages such as being a minority, a woman of improvised background, with language deficiency, and other challenges. I was prepared to make the Army my only career. It had been a good choice for me, and I saw no need to jump into another career that I knew little about. All this changed with my mother's visit in November 1987.

She arrived uncharacteristically early before my graduation, and so I questioned why she had come early to see me. She mentioned that time was running out, and that she needed to see me before she died. I thought at first, here we go again with another of my mom's dying stories. I seemed to have a mother that was dying once a week. So I joked with her at first about what was killing her this time. She remained serious and said softly, "Consuelo the time has come for me to join my God. Don't worry. I will be fine. You see *Mi Hija* (my daughter) when you have served God according to his will any day is a good day to die. I am not afraid to leave this world. However, I am afraid of what you will become so I have taken this opportunity to speak with you about my dying wish."

I felt my heart ache and tears begin to well up in my eyes. She gently looked at me and said, "Don't cry. I need you to be strong and listen to me because I have something very important to share with you. Let's take a walk."

I stepped outside my home and accompanied her down the sidewalk a few paces. She stopped me and asked me to

do something unusual. She said, "Take your shoes off and walk barefoot just like you did while growing up poor as a child."

I found this request awkward and definitely uncomfortable, especially because the souls of my feet were soft. As an adult, I was used to wearing shoes. I respected her request and as I found myself wobbling trying to keep my feet firm on the ground, she told me about her dying wish. She pointed out that I had lost my footing on the ground because I had forgotten who I was. Now that I lived a better life, I seemed to take life too casually and in her words, "seemed to have little regard for others."

She asked me what at first seemed like a silly question. She asked me if I believed I was a leader. I had a wall full of decorations and awards, and my mother dared to ask such a silly question! I responded somewhat sarcastically, "Of course, Mom, I am a leader. Didn't you see my wall of decorations and certificates? You must agree that I have come a long way. You know what my life was like since I was born and raised in a *barrio* (ghetto) back in Laredo, Texas."

She responded, "Yes, I know how hard you have worked to become the successful person you have become. But, in my eyes, you have yet to become a leader among leaders."

She was talking about becoming a servant leader, a concept I didn't necessarily understand at the time. She defined servant leadership as the passing on to others of that which you have learned, and taking greater pride in seeing others succeed even if it means that they surpass you. She called servant leadership a shared leadership whereby you accept that what you do is never about you, but rather about the people you serve. She went on to say that while I had accomplished much and had come a long way, my journey

was just beginning. She wanted me to promise her before she died that when the day came, I would return home to become a role model for children and families. (She added that I would be spiritually guided.) She felt incredible sadness at the state of affairs young people were finding themselves in, and she believed in her heart that I had the right message of hope and inspiration for young people. She pleaded with me that children were hurting today in our society, and that children were basically good and wonderful. She considered children today as being lonely and confused. She wanted me to be there for children and their families. She wanted me to work with teachers and agencies advocating for children.

I knew her requests were way off my present career path, and I didn't understand why my mother would leave me with this great task. Me, motivate kids and help them? I asked my mother just how she envisioned I would be able to reach out to kids.

She answered, "Don't worry. Just trust God to guide you and you will be fine."

We kept walking and finally turned around to come inside. My mother left a few days later and within two weeks she passed away suddenly after what was to be a simple corrective surgery. Somehow, she knew—and now I *knew* what had to be done. It was the "when I had to do it" dilemma that troubled me. Feeling unqualified to help kids, I remained in the Army for another nine years.

In 1995, I received the phone call all career officers wait for, the notification that you made the commander's list. I spoke with a high ranking officer who congratulated me on my selection and basically told me I now had a good chance to compete for the ultimate step to become a full colonel, which positioned me for General. It's every officer's dream

to retire as a general. It was at this crucial time that my mother's words came back to me and with a calm I cannot to this day explain, I requested to be retired from the U. S. Army.

You can imagine how confused and perplexed the Army was at my decision to walk away from the greatest opportunity in my Army career. To do what? I told the Army I would still be serving our country only this time I would prepare tomorrow's leaders - our children. The Army granted my wish to retire, and in February 1996 I began to fulfill my mother's dying wish – to reach out to children.

As I write this book, it has been seven years since I started my journey, and I have been able to reach out to more than one million kids across America and Mexico. This book is about what I have learned from kids because kids have educated me as well. I will be sharing their stories along with mine and offering you, the young reader, the opportunity to take a journey with me by reading this book. I thank you for taking this step to read this heartfelt book about life, it's choices, driving toward your destiny by following a roadmap to success.

I hope and pray it will be a companion of goodwill, motivation, inspiration, and knowledge to you. It is with the best intentions to serve you, the young reader, that I offer what I believe to be a realistic look at what's going on in a world where young people must live, work, go to school, find happiness and make their own contributions. Thank you for helping a daughter make a dying mother's wish come true. You are the beneficiaries of that wish, and I believe she is watching from Heaven now with an angelic smile on her face.

Consuelo

Introduction

What are the rules to the game of life? Why does the world seem so unfair? What can I do to make better decisions? What am I supposed to do with my life? Why was I born? Who am I? How can I use the talents and skills people tell me I have to make something of myself? Why do some people become more successful than others?

I've thought about all these questions at one time or another, as a teenager, young adult and as an adult. It really would have saved me a lot of time and trouble if there had been something I could have read to help me roadmap my success. Life is a journey, so why haven't there been more readable signposts along the way, especially for young people?

The book you are now holding is an answer to that question. I have written it to help teenagers specifically, and parents and teachers in general. This is the book I wish someone had handed me when I was 16 so I could have gotten a head start on my success in life. It describes the core values that we must have to live a happy, healthy and successful life. It explains how our life is built around the choices we make and how those choices determine our success or failure in life.

One of the important choices you can make is whether or not you are going to read this book. I've even asked myself

if I would have read this book when I was a 16-year-old. Would I have started it, gotten 20 or 30 pages into it, and stopped reading? Would I have picked it up and leafed through it a couple of times before I decided I wasn't worth the effort? Knowing the type of teen I was, there's a 50-50 chance that might have happened. I'd like to think I would have cared about myself enough to read it.

I'm going to ask you to be smarter—and wiser—than that. Take a chance on your growth and development by taking a chance on this book. Read it from cover-to-cover. Make notes in the margins. Highlight meaningful passages. Talk to your friends. Talk to teachers. Ask your parents for their perspective. Show people this book and discuss important insights. Allow the stories, true life examples and suggestions in this book to help you make better decisions and life-enriching choices.

I hope something you read will help you see how the world works, and how special—and needed—you are, so you find your place in the world more quickly and more happily. It took years for me to find my place. I grew up in my little village in Laredo, Texas, where I never envisioned the life I have today. It was difficult to dream then. I lived with my seven brothers, two sisters, my mother and my father in what was called, El Rincon del Diablo (The Devil's Den). It was the place that tourists coming to our border city were warned about. But my village (the *barrio*, as it is called today) sustained me in many ways that I have come to appreciate. While life has provided me with many lessons, living in my *barrio* provided me with basic values and traditions that I now recognize as the framework for my success in life.

We must believe in ourselves, feel that we will be okay no matter what comes along. I now know I lacked an ability to

champion myself. A mentor, a supporting parent, a caring teacher are all gems to treasure—don't waste the opportunity to learn from them, for they are very special to us. I urge you to cultivate, embrace and appreciate those individuals.

This book encourages you to sift through all the messages you get about being a boy or girl, and becoming a man or woman, to throw out what you believe is not you, find the real you, and—most importantly—be happy with who you are. Life has its surprises, disappointments and loss opportunities, but it also has its spectacular moments, crowning achievements and joys.

Embrace life. Cherish its goodness. I firmly believe that if you were to take a personal inventory, you would realize that you have much more to be grateful for than you think. You are alive and reading this book. I have written it for you. I have written it to give you a better start than I had. Finding answers through discussion of who we are and what we want to be is the framework of a mature, secure person. In this book, my goal is to have young people plan ahead. If I had to live my life again, what would I have wanted to know 25-30 years ago?

I realize you are growing up in a world different from the one I experienced. We live in the 21st Century now. The economy, jobs, technology, schools, families, the military and religious institutions have undergone catastrophic changes. In the post-911 era, America is not the same America. In the midst of all this unnerving change, there is one thing that has not changed—the core values of highly successful and happy people. I want you to inherit those core values. They are the values that will sustain you, protect you and guide you through life, no matter what circumstances you find yourself in or challenges you face.

Introduction

The core values listed below will not only help you achieve the life you want, they will help you become a better person. They are both your "sails" and your "anchors." They will carry you swiftly toward your dreams and become a source of stability for you during trials, tribulations and storms.

Through my own trials and tribulations, I have come to believe that there is a special set of core values that determines our success or failure in life. In an effort to frame this book, I will speak about these core values. I believe these core values are the basis for who we are and what we become as we go through life. I have named a chapter after each of these values to both organize and simplify your reading. Although each chapter stands on its own, there are certain linkages and story synopses that will be missed unless you read the chapters in the order they appear. However, you are welcome to start anywhere in the book, knowing that each chapter will fulfill its purpose.

The chapters in the order they appear are: Identity; Attitude; Humility and Compassion; Gratitude; Honesty and Integrity; Motivation and Confidence; Respect; Responsibility; Work Ethic; Self-Discipline; Creativity; Ethics and Morals; Faith in Positive Outcomes; and Duty, Honor and Country.

I invite you to spend quality time with this book. Refuse to neglect your growth and development. Visit each of these chapters with the idea that you will learn something about yourself—and about life itself. Read with an open mind and a willing heart. Have the courage to follow the recommendations and actions I suggest throughout the book. Don't do it for me—do it for yourself!

There is something I want you to remember as you read this book. It is the advice my parents gave me whenever I doubted my abilities or was told I could not achieve some-

thing that meant a lot to me. Whenever I used the word "can't," my parents would say *Porque No*—Why Not? So, I will pass that advice on to you. The next time you hear someone say, "You can't" or use that expression yourself to avoid taking a risk or testing your own ability, ask *Porque No?*

Will you take the lessons in this book to heart? *Porque No?* Can you be all you are meant to be? *Porque No?* Will you be a good role model for others to follow? *Porque No?* Can you keep a positive attitude and a strong work ethic? *Porque No?* Will you practice self-discipline and use your creativity? *Porque No?* Although you may want more things, are you grateful for what you have? *Porque No?* Are you willing to invest in yourself and go for your dream? *Porque No?* Will you give a retired Lieutenant Colonel a chance to make a difference in your life? *Porque No?*

Through a collage of stories, personal experiences, facts, inspiration and humor, this book will help you discover and appreciate your own uniqueness. If I can help you do that, I will feel as if I have honored the memory of my parents and put you in a position to achieve extraordinary success if life. Drop me a note or e-mail me. I would love to hear from you.

The correct and harmonious course of action is always to be found in us if we are in touch with ourselves.   [Gayle High Pine]

We cannot afford to think about who is getting ahead of us and how they don't deserve it. The desire to be better than someone else can choke off the simple desire to be yourself.
[Julia Cameron]

Remember that life is a work in progress and that you are a H-I-T — a Human-In-Training.
[Dan Millman]

Chapter 1

Identity

Shine the inside so the outside can sparkle.

A big part of coming up with a strategy for managing our lives is knowing who we are and how we feel about some important dimensions of living. I'm going to start right off by telling you the theme for this chapter: *You can't know where you're going until you know who you are!* That statement is as true now as it was 50,000 years ago. The challenge is for each and every single one of us to discover and then express our own special uniqueness.

This means understanding who we are—and who we aren't. Growing into the person we are meant to be is our chief responsibility in life. Expressing our uniqueness is critical to our success because it authenticates our life's journey and justifies the contributions we are meant to make. Otherwise, we will go through life rudderless, cast adrift on the sea of life, carried by currents of fear, doubt, anger, guilt and hopelessness.

Our individual identity is the foundation of our being. We are created with a special purpose, and have been given all the things we need to fulfill that purpose. How we express our individual identity is the ultimate statement of who we are. Remember: *we can't know where we are going until we know who we are*. So, it is important for us to nurture our nature and to be who we are.

Allen Funt, the originator of "Candid Camera," loved to catch people being themselves. He particularly enjoyed learning from children. "Children are beautiful," he said, "They're so original, so independent. They're everything you wish adults were. But adults are constantly hard-minded, conformant and subject to bowing to group pressure. They're moving away from individualism toward the herd."

To prove his point, Funt contrasts two film clips from "Candid Camera" episodes. One clip shows a man walking up a down escalator. He is followed by another customer who also walks up the down escalator. A few moments later a woman follows suit. Several more customers mindlessly do the same thing a short while later.

The second clip captures children's behavior. I'll let Allen Funt tell the story: "A child walks up to a large, empty box. He inspects it carefully, decides it's a fortress. He gets into it and shoots away at an imaginary enemy. Another child strolls up to the box the previous child is vacating. She decides it's a house, gets into it and plays grown-up. A third child sees the previous child's antics and approaches the

same box. But he decides it's a roller coaster and gleefully slides it down an incline nearby..."

As these series of clips show, too many adults fail to take advantage of opportunities to express their true nature. Children have absolutely no difficulty doing it. Expressing our own uniqueness and individuality is our birthright. The sooner we give ourselves permission to cultivate our own personality, the better.

Many of us chase after slippery ideals that are forced upon us by well-meaning people and organizations who haven't taken time to know us or understand us. We want to be loved and accepted, so we believe we must change who we are to match other people's expectations of us. We say things like: "As soon as I lose this excess weight, I'll be able to be successful" or "Once my acne clears up, I'll get the perfect boyfriend or girlfriend" or "If I buy my friend's things, they'll hang with me longer" or "If I do drugs and drink with my friends, they'll respect me and look out for me."

Rather than striving to fit someone else's preconceived ideas of who and what we should be or how we should look, we can choose to appreciate ourselves now. We can celebrate our own uniqueness, our own special weight, height and hair color, our own ethnic heritage.

Robert Schuller's story about the ten-inch frying pan reminds us of one of the chief reasons people fail to express their true uniqueness. If you haven't heard it, you're in for a treat. If you have heard it, it's worth repeating.

A tourist walked down a pier and watched a fisherman reel in a large fish, measure it and throw it back into the bay. He caught a second fish which was smaller than the first catch, but kept it and put it in his bucket. The tourist watched several more sequences of catches in which the larger fish were tossed back and the smaller fish were kept.

Puzzled, the curious on-looker approached the fisherman.

"Pardon me, I couldn't help notice that you're keeping the small fish and throwing the large fish back. Shouldn't it be the other way around?"

The fisherman looked up and without blinking an eye responded, "Heavens no! My frying pan only measures ten inches across."

Before you judge the fisherman too harshly, how many people do you know who have that same ten-inch frying pan mentality? How many times do your friends limit their ability to dream big because they are thinking too small? How many times do you do it to yourself? Norman Vincent Peale described it this way:

There is a deep tendency in human nature to become precisely what we imagine or picture ourselves to be. We tend to equate with our own self-appraisal of either depreciation or appreciation. We determine either self-limitation or unlimited growth potential.

Young people who limit themselves through "frying pan" thinking usually project negative thoughts which bring negative consequences. People who have a passion for success think beyond the limitations imposed by frying pans.

They see the larger picture. They know they can alter the size of the pan to accommodate the size of their dreams! Their passion to succeed lifts them to higher levels of commitment, enthusiasm and self-expression.

The fisherman in the above story failed to ask IF questions: What *if* the pan is too small? What *if* I keep the large fish and toss the smaller ones back? *If* I keep the larger fish, I could cut my fishing time in half, couldn't I? *If* I cut the larger fish in half, I could have twice as many meals.

The interesting thing about the word *if* is that it appears in the center of the word *life:* L-i-f-e. The center of the word representing our very existence is *iffy. Iffiness* underscores our everyday thoughts, feelings and actions. "*If* I do this" or "*If* I do that" or "*If* this happens" or "*If* only I had done this instead of that, gone here instead of there, or stopped then instead of now." Life is full of *ifs*–or at least half of life is. The *iffy* part of life may be filled with uncertainties and doubt, but the other half of life brings us certainties, stability and direction.

What *if* we really knew ourselves? What *if* we truly appreciated our talents and abilities? What would happen *if* we stood up for our principles and core values? What *if* we forgave people who have wronged us? What *if* we could do something all over again—what would we do?

It is the *if* side of life, the risky side of life that stretches us and causes us to experiment and to grow. "*If* I can do this, maybe I can do that;" or "I believe I can succeed at this *if* I do this;" or "*If* I have a passion to succeed, I wonder how many doors will open for me?"

Many young people eat, sleep and live on the *iffy* side of life. One of the toughest situations I come across at student assemblies is when young people tell me they are adopted and do not know who they are. I tell them it's okay to ask questions. While you may not accept foster parenting or adoption, the important thing is that you belong—you are wanted. Many of you tell me you feel incomplete because your siblings are not biological siblings. Yet being connected biologically is not a guarantee of closeness or brotherly/sisterly love.

Dear Colonel Kickbusch:

I attended your 9th grade presentation at South High yesterday. I sat in the front row and was able to see all the facial expressions and tears. The stories about your mother made me think of mine. When I went home I helped her out around the house by doing laundry, dishes and many other things. She had surgery and was in a lot of pain. Your stories helped me realize that just because she's mom doesn't mean she is responsible to do everything. I enjoyed all of your stories, especially the ones about your "home boys." They were hilarious! Thank you for taking the time to speak with us.

Sincerely,

Kate

Some of you are ashamed of your parents for various reasons: they don't speak English well (or not at all), they are not well educated, or they are poor. There's the trauma of having parents who are alcoholic, child abusers, drug addicts or sexual predators. Some young people come from immigrant parents, who may not speak English well or be formally educated, but they would give their lives for their child. Others may live with a single mother, but I believe this is still a family. (I mention the single-mother household because these outnumber the single-father households; however, I am aware of the gaping hole a motherless home can have as well). You should not feel out of place, because, unfortunately there are many broken homes.

Sometimes our schools are not sensitive to the many situations that young people from single parent households face, such as the Father/Daughter Banquet, the Father/Son Football Night, the Mother/Daughter Luncheon, the Mother/Son Sports Luncheon, and so on. A friend told me of an incident that I cannot help but share.

During a homecoming football game, players and their parents were announced as they crossed the field to the cheering of the crowd. My friend watched as a young man crossed the football field. He held his head low as his name was announced. There was no parent or adult by his side. How alone that young man must have felt. My heart aches even now as I envision that young man cross that field alone. I wish I could somehow have been there for him, to accompany him so he could have held his head high.

In another instance, a school held its yearly Father/Daughter Luncheon. A good friend of mine had just enrolled her daughter as a freshman in a private school. This young lady's father had died when she was in the second grade, and she was still struggling with her loss. When she learned of this "tradition" at the school the pain resurfaced, prompting her not to want to attend school the day of the banquet. She identified herself with the loss of her parent, and the school failed to see the predicament they had placed her in.

So how do we deal with these situations? One way is to refuse to feel incomplete with what we don't have. Take your mother to the banquet, your father to the luncheon, invite your grandparents, a good family friend, an aunt or an uncle or your favorite teacher. And don't feel embarrassed about these situations. Speak to school officials and you can sensitize them to different situations and together find alternatives.

It seems today that image and acceptance by others or our peers is critical in young lives. I believe that while it is important to take care of external needs, it is more important to realize that what is inside is what's critically important. What's inside is what gives you the character to move ahead.

I still remember the impeccably dressed professional woman who came up to me at a conference and said: "Look at me right now in my $500 dress, $200 shoes, fine expensive jewelry! Yet, I feel like $1.99." What was she saying? I believe she meant that she did not "find" herself by what

she bought. She was trying to find her authentic self, her self-esteem, her self-worth and her self-confidence. While a designer dress or expensive jewelry can make you feel good, that kind of feeling is only temporary. What happens when styles change—when "Tommy" is no longer the "in" thing? When the "Dooney" is not "where it's at?" It's back to square one! What do you have left? How much of you is the real you?

So, WHO ARE YOU? How much of your initiative, inspiration, strength, and commitment come from within? What are your personal values? Are you real or counterfeit? These are important questions to ask yourself. It is important to discover these answers for yourself and to believe that those answers are the right ones for you. If you cannot define yourself, someone else will define you. And they may be entirely incorrect about who you are and present you to others as someone they define. Do not let anyone else define who you are!

I agree with Swiss psychologist Carl Jung who said:

People will do anything, no matter how absurd, in order to avoid facing their [true selves.]. They will practice yoga and all its exercises, observe a strict regimen of diet, learn theosophy by heart, or mechanically repeat mystic texts from the literature of the...world—all because they cannot get on with themselves and have not the slightest faith that anything useful could ever come out of their own [lives].

Many of the boys and girls in the world in which I grew up believed they would never amount to anything. Like the woman in the $500 dress I mentioned earlier, they believed they were worth only $1.99. One of my childhood experiences helped me to understand the difference in our net-worth and our self-worth.

I was 12 years old and had no idea that I lived in a poor neighborhood. The word poor had never been mentioned in my home. I was asked by my mother to go "uptown," to the other side of the tracks, to run an errand for her. She told me explicitly to take bus number 34 and to behave in a respectful manner.

"Remember," she said, "you come from a good family with good values, so don't do anything to bring shame to our family."

I did what I was supposed to do and was waiting for the bus at the bus stop. I sat on the bench and saw what I believed to be the most beautiful woman in the world. Today, I jokingly say that beautiful people look like French poodles. They are dressed up and cute-looking. She had fingernail polish that matched her clothes. I never had seen a woman so nicely dressed and accessorized.

My lovely mother smelled like cilantro and garlic most of the time. She was not a professional woman with an income that could afford her luxury cosmetics or clothing. I was dressed in what back home is called "Segunda." A "Segunda" is a 25- cent dress that my mother, who had a keen eye for good fabric, would say was a really good deal. My mother would select second-hand clothes from piles of clothing donated by people from up north to the less advan-taged people along the border.

The beautiful woman at the bus stop noticed me, espe-cially since I was watching her with my mouth open. Well, I couldn't help it. I was impressed to see all the shiny jew-elry she was wearing. She asked me my name and where I

lived. I responded with such pride, "Vengo del Rincon del Diablo" meaning "I am from the devils den!"

She must have known this was a tough neighborhood, because her response was apathetic, sympathetic, empathetic—I'm not sure which of the pathetics it was. She said, "You poor thing" and immediately distanced herself from me by getting onto her bus. I was stunned to hear someone say I was poor.

I thought I had learned something my father did not know and decided to surprise my parents with the new information I had obtained. I ran to the backyard where my father was tending to the chickens and yelled, "Father, hurry—come and listen to what I just learned!"

He paused and told me to calm down. Then he washed his hands and stepped out of the chicken coop to sit down on a bench he had made under a big orange tree. I told him gleefully, "Guess what, we are poor!"

"What did you say?" he responded.

I replied, "See. You did not even know we were poor! I know something you did not know!"

My father, with that beautiful calm voice and tenderness he always showed me, taught me then the difference between net-worth and self-worth. He said, "We are not poor. We don't have the material things that people often choose as the most important way to identify people. But we are rich. Rich in culture, values, traditions and a faith that all people are equal. As long as you work hard, have integrity, and believe in the American dream, you can become whatever you want to be in life. You will learn from your struggles and experiences. Poverty helps build character, hope and determination in people. I will not allow anyone in my fam-

ily to think poorly, act poorly, or behave poorly. Do you understand?"

I remember nodding my understanding, and recognizing how fortunate I was to have such a wise father.

If you feel shame because you don't wear designer clothes, live in a big house, drive a nice car or have an endless amount of money to spend, it's time to change your thinking! Don't shortchange yourself. Material wealth pales in comparison when it comes to inner riches.

For you, the young reader who may already be blessed with nice clothes, new car, nice big home, and money to spend, remember that things may make you happy in the short run, but inner wealth is a permanent wealth. It will make you happy in the long run. Finding success is about working within yourself and feeling priceless rather than wearing expensive clothes and feeling like $1.99! Trust me, many people who live surrounded by material wealth live tormented lives because they confuse their self-worth with their net-worth.

Most people underestimate themselves and fail to see how truly unique they are. They overlook their talents and abilities, and lose many opportunities for personal and professional growth. Whatever we do, we must be true to our calling. In the words of missionary Pearl S. Buck, "A writer must write, a dancer must dance, a painter must paint and a musician must play." If we do not joyfully express who we are, we will live incomplete lives.

We are all answerable to ourselves. We are irrevocably tied to our own living biographies. One of my roles as a professional speaker is to help young people realize and express their own richness and uniqueness. This next state-

ment might be one of the most important pieces of guidance in this nook, so read it carefully. You may want to read it a second time—it's that important. Here it is: You are painting a portrait of yourself every time you think, feel and act. Each situation and circumstance you find yourself in is your canvas. Your core values are your brushes. What you paint is up to you. I speak from personal experience when I say that the more consistent you are in matching the brush strokes with the core values in this book, the more colorful, vibrant and beautiful your masterpiece will be. And that masterpiece is your life.

What kind of life are you painting every day? Are you painting your picture or someone else's? Is the finished result you or an imitation of someone else? I encourage you to be you. Be true. Make it happen! Maybe that's why you're not going where you want to go—be who you want to be. I see young people who know they are going in the wrong direction with drug use, early sexual activity, lying to parents. But they delude themselves into thinking they can make it up the next time. How many "first times" do we hear about? "I got pregnant the first time I had sex," or " I only took the drug once," or "It was the first time I shot a gun." It only takes the "first time" to ruin young lives and devastate families. Having core values is a way to empower yourself against many "first times" in the face of peer pressure.

Core values provide a way to improve life, and to provide better values. They provide hope and faith that you can embrace as a way of living. So, become core value #1—Be yourself. Enjoy being who you are. Be authentically you. Develop your talents and abilities. Express your uniqueness. Everyone has talent. I have never met a person who does not have some kind of talent, even if it wasn't apparent to them. Some people are certainly more gifted than others in certain areas. One person's talent may lie in singing, while another individual is an amazing sculptor. Other people are talented in the area of medicine, mathematics, chemistry or science. Some people can out-jump, out-run, out-climb and out-smart others.

All of us have special gifts, but some of us discount them or take them for granted for any number of reasons. Others, like Michael Jordan, appreciate their talents and use them. "If you have done your best," he said, "then you will have had some accomplishments along the way. Not everyone is going to be the greatest basketball player, but you can still be considered one of the best at what you do." He knew who he was and expressed who he was—and so can you.

Reflection Exercises

1. Read each statement and answer it by filling in the blanks next to it. This exercise is designed to provide an opportunity for you to practice thinking about your identity—what it is and how to develop it to its full potential.

> I am … *a human being.*
> I am … *a son/daughter/sister/brother.*
> I am … *very good with math problems.*
> I am …
> I am …
> I am …

2. If you were going to tell yourself exactly who you are each day when you get up, what would you say?

3. Those who are successful speak well of themselves to themselves. Make a list of statements you can make about yourself each day.

> ❖ Today I will remember to say thank you to those who help me.
> ❖ I will learn a new word and use it in a conversation.
> ❖
> ❖
> ❖

4. Core values exercise: Write a brief paragraph about why it is important to know who you are (based on identity as a core value).

5. From whom do you learn? Who is important in your life? Using the chart on the next page, name some people you admire, and explain why. I've started with a few examples, so you understand what to do.

PERSON I ADMIRE	BECAUSE
Mrs. K	*She is a good leader.*
John Doe	*He knows who he is.*
Mrs. R.	*She is proud of who she is.*
Miss C.	*She treats me with respect.*

If you have to walk alone, so be it!
Just know yourself.

You can complain because roses have thorns, or you can rejoice because thorns have roses.
[Ziggy]

It is our attitude, not our aptitude, that determines our altitude.   *Robert Schuller]*

What a wonderful life I've had. Only I wish I realized it sooner.   *[Collette]*

Chapter 2

Attitude

Choose the "Midas Touch"
instead of the "Minus Touch."

I hear so many young people say to me: "He had *attitude*…that's why I beat him up!" or "She was showing me *attitude,* so I had to take care of her and I slapped her." We refer to people as having *attitude* in the way they dress themselves, or *attitude* in the way they speak, or attitude in the way they behave.

However, the *attitude* we are referring to here is not that kind of "in your face, look at me" *attitude*. Attitude is about how we approach situations or events—our mental or moral disposition. We can have a positive or a negative attitude. The above examples imply a negative attitude.

Negative attitudes seem more prevalent today because of how we use the word.

If you want to benefit from using the "Midas Touch" instead of the "Minus Touch," positive attitudes are the key. Jay McGraw, author of *Daily Life Strategies for Teens*, puts it this way:

> *If you want to start taking real control of your life and start making better decisions instead of repeating attitudes you know are not good for you—(attitudes) that ultimately ruin your self-esteem and threaten your safety—then you've got to figure out what "influences" are making you screw up so badly. Connect the dots between your self-defeating (attitudes) and the payoffs you are getting from these attitudes.*

Attitudes are powerful human responses to what happens in the world around you. Our attitude speaks for us even before we open our mouths. Attitude is important in how we approach life. A positive attitude makes those around us want to be with us. A positive attitude for a student in school makes teachers more approachable. Teachers enjoy helping students with positive attitudes. This positive attitude is evidenced when we have our homework assignments done neatly and turned in on time. If we turn in a paper that is dirty, with erasures or full of corrections we are showing a negative attitude.

Likewise, the boss who has an employee with a positive attitude will be more likely to help him or her succeed at work. Coming in late, leaving early, and taking longer lunches are signs of a negative attitude that will surely get the boss's attention—unfortunately, it will be negative attention!

A parent will be more likely to extend a curfew for a special occasion when the son or daughter has met the curfew without fail on other occasions. This shows the parent that the son or daughter is responsible and has a good attitude about the house rules. Doing assigned chores around the house with a positive attitude is more likely to influence the parent to give permission to the son or daughter for other activities.

A good friend of mine, Jimmy Cabrera, professional speaker and author of *What's In Your Backpack?*, showed a group of students a really neat way to look at attitude. Here's how he describes it:

> *Although the following statement has been around for a long time, it has much to say about the nature of success: Attitude is everything. 'Everything' means 100 percent of something. Right! Using the 26-letter English alphabet to help make my point, I am going to (organize the word "attitude" alphabetically). Each letter of the alphabet has a corresponding number. A is the first letter, so it gets a 1; Z is the 26th letter, so it equals the number 26. Let's complete the equation for the word 'attitude:'*

$$A(1) + T(20) + T(20) + I(9) + T(20) + U(21) + D(4) + E(5) = 100\%$$

Attitude really is everything when it comes to processing human experience. You may know a guy who's a serious jerk, or a girl who's narcissistically self-absorbed, or a teacher who's unnecessarily hurtful, or a parent who won't listen. But the problem arises if you start seeing those negative experiences through negative attitudinal filters.

For example, if you live with parents or guardians that leave little room for discussion or two-way communication

between themselves and their kids, it doesn't take long for teenagers to get an *attitude* that says "what's the sense of even talking with your parents or guardians?" You may add, "They are going to go about doing things their own way and never mind what I think or feel about anything." I would encourage you to find family members who do listen and use them as sounding boards and buffers. If you feel no one out there is really willing to listen, I encourage you to write about your thoughts. This technique is called journaling. It's a great way to release your thoughts and frustrations without upsetting or hurting someone else. Journaling takes effort on your part to record what you feel, what happened to you, ideas you don't want to forget, attitudes you want to change or adopt, or simply your impression of the day.

Journaling can lead to many good things. It releases tension and allows you to reflect on your feelings, thoughts and attitudes. It becomes a great stress releaser and cathartic technique, especially when you are feeling anger or pain. Journaling is like having a best friend around whenever you need one. One nice thing about having a journal as your best friend is that while it won't talk back to you, it will repeat what you have said—so you have a chance for reflection and corrective action.

Some of you have already experienced great tragedies in your young lives. Perhaps you don't think things can get any worse, and you feel entitled to have an attitude of distrust and fear about people—especially when those in your past may have hurt you. I feel compelled to share with you something very personal that happened to me which caused me to adopt an attitude of distrust towards adults. The life-changing event occurred when I was a mere nine years old.

My mother sent me across the street to deliver a plate of food for our neighbors. They were an elderly couple that my parents respected and trusted. On this dreadful day, I entered their home with the idea of simply giving them the dish my mother had sent. I found myself in the living room with just the husband. He began to touch me in places I felt awkward about and I became frightened. He told me to keep quiet and threatened to tell my mother that I had been a bad little girl. He assured me my mother would spank me for misbehaving in someone else's house. He knew my mother was a strict disciplinarian. I told him I would not tell anyone.

He touched me inappropriately on other occasions. Little did I know that this type of abuse would not stop with him. Two other elderly men eventually abused me. All threatened me by saying they would accuse me of misbehaving, and make sure my mother would beat me. I lived in my own personal little hell for three years until the fondling stopped. It took another ten years—when I was leaving for college—for me to understand what had happened to me. I felt ashamed and dirty. I did not know this was sexual abuse and that it was not my fault. It took a long time before I was finally able to regain the trust I had lost with adults, especially older men.

I had difficulty with relationships because I developed an attitude that I did not deserve to be loved or cared for. I felt I was not worthy, since I had experienced such a horrible life as a child. I wish I had had someone to encourage me to report the abuse and get help. I let unscrupulous, unprincipled, immoral old men abuse me and take advantage of my innocence. Although it still bothers me from

time to time, I realize it is part of my past—and my past, anyone's past, doesn't have to be a life sentence. I am a firm believer in the fact that none of us should have to live in torment for years because we feel no one will understand or listen to us, or we fear they will judge us harshly for a traumatic childhood experience.

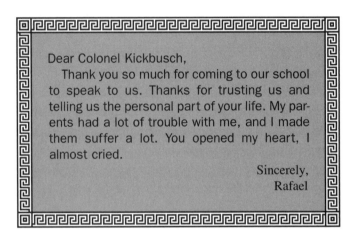

Dear Colonel Kickbusch,

Thank you so much for coming to our school to speak to us. Thanks for trusting us and telling us the personal part of your life. My parents had a lot of trouble with me, and I made them suffer a lot. You opened my heart, I almost cried.

Sincerely,
Rafael

If you are involved in a desperate situation like child abuse, drugs, depression, sexual abuse or mental abuse, please seek help immediately. Start by letting your school counselor or social worker know. These individuals can provide the professional help and guidance you need immediately. If you feel that your counselor or social worker cannot help, call the local number in the yellow pages for child protective services. These people are highly skilled professionals. They can get you help right away.

If you have friends who seem chronically despondent, depressed or angry, don't judge them right away. Instead ask what's going on. Let your friend know that you know they have changed, that he or she doesn't seem like himself

or herself. Ask your friend what I call leading questions. For example:

- ❖ I notice you're feeling down lately. Are things okay at home?
- ❖ I notice you have been getting a little short on temper. What's going on that seems to cause you so much anger lately?
- ❖ You don't feel like doing much anymore like talking on the phone, hanging out or going out with your old friends. Is there something we have done that has caused you to avoid us?
- ❖ I am aware there is a divorce going on with your parents. Would you like to talk to me about your feelings? I may not have the answers but at least I am here to be a friend.
- ❖ I am sorry to hear about the death in your family. While I can't help ease the pain, I am here to offer you my compassion and sympathy. I care about you very much.

I believe that for every bad encounter, there is also a good one we need to remember or seek in order to avoid getting a negative attitude. If nothing else, think positive thoughts or hang on to a special song that brings joy to your life. Read a poem that lifts your spirits. Write to the friend that you know will help you get through the tough times.

Again, I can't say enough about journaling and how helpful it is. Any notebook or binder with paper will do. The important thing is that you don't keep pain or anger inside. Use some outlet, like a friend or journal, to vent your pain or anger in a controlled and therapeutic way. We are blessed with giving ourselves the greatest gift of all: we can change

our life circumstances—immediately—by changing our attitude! I find it funny when I hear people debate whether a glass is half empty or half full. My response is: Who cares? Fill it up with joy, hope, and love.

We cannot be happy and sad at the same time. We cannot feel peaceful and frightened at the same time. We cannot be confident and doubtful in the same breath. We cannot be angry and compassionate at the same time. It is impossible for us to be optimistic and pessimistic at the same time. We can choose the "Midas Touch" or the "Minus Touch."

I am sure that it will come as no surprise to you that when you are living in a time of personal crisis, economic downturns and overall negative circumstances, your attitude and behavior will feel the effects of the pressure. You move cautiously through each day, and may even feel emotionally drained, which keeps you out-of-sync and out-of-sorts.

I can also attest that once you believe you have made the turn toward recovery and recuperation, your attitudes tend to become more positive and hopeful. When we "roll with the punches" we find that we can rewrite endings to match our positive attitudes. We view the changes we make as opportunities, not threats.

Without overlooking the seriousness of some of the obstacles we have overcome or currently face, I encourage you to experiment with the changes you know you must make to live a more enriched, balanced, joyful and productive life. The attitudes you have today create the future you want tomorrow. You may want to read that last sentence again, because it's central to the understanding of and appreciation for how well you do in life. "People are always blaming their circumstances," said George Bernard Shaw. "The people who get on in this world are the people who get up and look for the circumstances they want, and if they can't find them, they invent them through (positive attitudes)."

Don't be afraid to be known as a person who champions a positive attitude and sees every circumstance as an opportunity for personal or professional growth. In Daryl Ott Underhill's book, *Every Woman Has a Story,* there's a quote: "We cannot become what we need to be by cultivating negative attitudes." When I read that, I knew I had to share it with you. It reminded me of the well-known story about a young teacher who couldn't become what he wanted to be because he cultivated a "know-it-all" attitude:

The young teacher decided to visit a wise old retired principal who had a similar specialty. The young teacher was writing a book and wanted to ask his old mentor a few questions and discuss several curiosities.

The old man received the self-assured teacher in his library, and an attendant served tea. As soon as the young teacher seated himself, he began boasting about his academic success, his considerable administrative credentials and his expertise in their shared field. The old principal said nothing as he poured tea into his boastful guest's cup. The young teacher hardly noticed the old doctor's hospitality and kept talking about his own accomplishments.

Suddenly the young teacher realized that his host was still pouring tea into an already overflowing cup. The hot tea was spilling over the table and onto the hardwood floor.

"Stop," cried the young teacher. "What are you doing? You're spilling all of the tea."

The retired principal looked at his puzzled colleague and smiled softly.

*"Just as the cup cannot hold anymore tea once it's filled,"
he replied, "how can I give you the information you need
when your ego is so full?"*

*As the retired principal demonstrated so dramatically, we
cannot listen to anyone else's advice or wise counsel if we are
full of ourselves. The young teacher in this story seemed to
be "full of himself." He had victimized himself with a
"know-it-all" attitude. He didn't leave room for more information—or growth. His egotistical attitude was getting in
the way of any benefits he could derive from his meeting with
the old administrator.*

I think back to my darker days as a child who was sexually abused and wondered why any adult would
intentionally hurt a child. The reason is simply there are
people out there who are very sick and should never be
around kids. My gift to myself was to cultivate positive attitudes, to look forward to being a good person, to refuse to
feel dirty or ashamed, to find the courage to say in this book
something that needed to be said in order to help someone
else. Somehow I feel someone out there needs me to write
about this. On the other hand, every time I talk about this
painful part of my past, it helps me to heal and move on
with my life. I think of the new challenges children face
today, with so much on-line pornography, and chat rooms
that invite perfect strangers into their lives. I am reminded
of a young man who turned to such a stranger on-line one
day when he was not getting along with his parents. This
stranger pretended to be a sympathetic adult who wanted to

help him. He sent the boy an electronic airplane ticket to California, where he was waiting for him. The boy was eventually rescued, but not before he had been molested and tortured.

So, remember that attitude is very important. Think positive. Seek to improve your feelings and thoughts about yourself and others. If you know someone needs your support remember to ask leading questions instead of passing judgment. If you need someone to be there with you, don't be afraid to seek help right away. The sooner you get help, the sooner you can recover and move on with life by using positive attitudes as your constant and faithful ally.

Reflection Exercises

1. Attitude is something that we develop over time. It doesn't just happen. We must work on developing our attitude just as we work on developing other skills. The following statements are suggestions you might want to consider in order to stay focused on the positive instead of the negative side of daily events, people or places. Place a check mark by any of the statements that might work for you.

__ Do away with small problems quickly by addressing them first.

__ Take care of bigger problems by breaking them down into smaller parts.

__ When you think about what will happen on a given day, think about the good things that can happen.

__ When you think back on the events of the day, think about the things that went well.

__ Share your learning experiences about attitude with someone you care about.

__ Read books or magazine articles about having a positive attitude. Ask your librarian for help.

__ If there is something negative in your life over which you have no control, refuse to worry about it. It really is your choice.

__ Take a few minutes each day to think about how you will use your positive attitude.

__ Add some of your own suggestions:

2. Developing a positive attitude can be enhanced by how we talk. Complete the following exercise by reading each sentence and circling T if you believe the statement is true or F if you believe the statement is false. The author of this exercise is Elwood Chapman. She has provided additional information at the end of the exercise. Please complete the exercise before you read the author's note.

   T F Funny storytellers have, on the average, more positive perspectives than non-funny storytellers.

   T F Those who adhere to the policy "if you can't say something good about someone, don't say anything" usually have more positive attitudes than others.

   T F When a problem is involved, talking about it can be therapeutic to the talker.

   T F Excessive talkers often seem more negative than others.

   T F Happy conversations translate into positive thoughts; positive thoughts translate into happy conversations; both translate into more positive attitudes.

   T F Positive people deliberately feed their minds positive thoughts.

   T F The more you complain about your situation, the more negative your general attitude becomes.

   T F People who, through uplifting conversations, help others remain positive also help their own attitudes.

T F It is easier to talk yourself into a negative mood than to talk yourself out of one.

T F It is easier to think yourself into a negative mood than to think or talk yourself out of one.

(NOTE: Elwood Chapman believes all of the statements are true. The purpose of the exercise is to communicate the importance of what we talk about and how it affects how we think. Positive talk usually gives us a more positive focus on life.)

3. Who are some "positive people" you know or have heard about? Who are some "negative people" you know or have heard about? What are the differences between these people with regard to how they live, interact with others, the work they do, and their lifestyle. Use the following chart to help you think through this exercise.

Positive People:

Negative People:

Describe what these "positive people" say and do. What makes them "positive"?

Describe what these "negative people" say and do. What makes them "negative"?

Which of the "positive" behaviors listed above do you practice?

Which of the "negative" behaviors listed above do you practice?

Write a few lines about how you can improve on the positive behaviors and turn the negative behaviors into positive ones:

Be a champion for positive attitudes and see every circumstance as an opportunity for personal or professional growth.

It is [our] sympathy with all creatures that truly makes us human. Until [we] extend [our] circle of compassion to all living things, [we] will not find peace.   *[Albert Schweitzer]*

Compassion is the language which the deaf can hear and the blind can see. [Mark Twain]

No one is useless in the world who lightens the burden of others.   *[Charles Dickens]*

Chapter 3

Humility and Compassion

Give and accept acts of loving kindness.

Once there was a kind, humble and charitable man who never turned a needy person away. He held an esteemed position in his church and was one of the town's chief employers. Through a series of unforeseen circumstances, he lost his business, his home, his considerable investments and his worldly possessions. He moved to another town, but found himself reduced to begging and doing menial labor to exist.

One day a passerby said to him, "Why don't you ask the rich miser, Antonio, for some work? He always needs help, and will most likely take advantage of your need for work,

because people don't work for him very long. At least you won't have to beg for work anymore."

Another person said, "Let me warn you about him. He is abusive, cruel and demanding. Everybody hates him and nobody wants to work for him."

The poor man was in such need that he took the first person's advice and asked the miser for a job. He was offered the lowly task of personal servant. The old miser, true to his nature, was grouchy, demanding, insensitive and generally toxic. For many years the poor man ignored the insults and cruel behavior of the old miser. He remained a faithful servant and treated his employer with respect and compassion.

The townspeople would take the poor servant aside and criticize his willingness to allow himself to be abused and taken advantage of by the crusty old miser.

However, the servant would always say, "This is the only way I know how to treat others. It is my duty to be kind and to be a loyal employee."

There came a day when the miser fell gravely ill. When the doctors told him he did not have long to live, the miser called for his faithful servant.

"You have been a loyal, loving servant for many years. You have endured my insults, bad manners, aggravating taunts and childish fits without complaint or judgment. I acted this way because I felt everyone in town was scheming to part me from my riches. Forgive me for taking it out on you."

The servant started to speak, but the miser motioned for him to remain silent. He had more to say.

"You have been a decent, humble and honest employee. Before I die, to make amends with you and God, I am leaving my entire fortune to you."

The miser asked his attorney to draw up the papers and gave the servant the keys to his safe and safety deposit box. Shortly after that, the wealthy miser died.

This story, adapted from the old wisdom literature, serves to remind us of the power of kindness, even under the most difficult of circumstances. The servant felt the suffering of the miser despite the miser's hard exterior and toxic personality. Perhaps you've met people—classmates, teachers, guidance counselors, camp directors, principals—who act like the miser in the story I used to introduce this chapter. Oftentimes, when people act that way, they are concealing some kind of pain, disappointment in themselves or even fear. Like the old miser, they use their anger, detachment and obnoxious behavior to distance themselves from the very people who can help them.

As you reach out to people in the ways you can, they will feel your calmness, your compassion, your love, concern and understanding. Just by being who you are, you'll be a healing presence in their lives. On the other hand, maybe you are a person who uses "old miser tactics" to hide your hurt, guilt or disappointment in yourself and distrust with life. If you are, I encourage you to reach out to someone you trust and accept the help that person can give you. I'm going to trust you with an intimate glimpse into my

childhood. It will serve to emphasize the differences between "old miser tactics" and "kind servant philosophy."

My mother was a person who had a difficult time expressing emotions such as love, compassion, understanding, and patience. I learned that her inability to be emotional in a good way was due to her being an orphan who was raised in a strict and stern home. She was beaten as a child and thought beatings were the "method of choice" for raising children. Later in her life, to her credit, she realized that physical abuse was the worst way to treat children.

What parents often fail to understand is that children don't realize how busy their parents' lives are, and find themselves resentful toward emotionally, economically and ethically challenged parents. Are you, or any of your friends living in a similar situation? Do you resent your parents for not being there when you need them? Do you take offense when classmates or people in town call you names that hurt your feelings? Are you resentful about where you live?

I grew up in a *barrio* called *El Rincon del Diablo*. Translated it meant "The Devil's Corner." By the time I was a freshman in high school, the *barrio* was called El Tonto, which meant "The Dummy." That name was worse than *El Rincon del Diablo,* because people would ask me, "Eres tonta?" (Are you a dummy?)

When you are judged on where you live, you can't escape the stigma, name-calling or labels associated with your neighborhood. As a young girl, I saw people injecting heroin into their arms on street corners. There was no Boy's Club or YWCA. All you had was the street. My biggest challenge as a youth was not to let the street have me. You've probably heard of the fancy academic degree called Rhodes Scholar. Well, I was a "Roads Scholar" by the time I went to college. I had seen it all. Even before I earned my

high school diploma or graduated from college, I had my degree from the "School of Hard Knocks."

I've seen drug pushers give drugs to young people so they get hooked. Once they're addicted, the dealers have a captive audience to use their "products." I've seen drug deals go bad and addicts' lives turn for the worst. One of my friends, Danny Salas, was stabbed numerous times in front of my eyes. His girlfriend paid the price, too. She was found dead with needles in her arms.

I got quite an education—both inside and outside of school! It's one I won't recommend, but it's the kind of "schooling" that can make you or break you. Many kids chose hatred, violence, and drug and alcohol addiction as their way of dealing with a hostile environment. Some elected to be resentful, suspicious and paranoid. Others chose anger, isolation and fear to keep the forces of evil at bay.

I was fortunate to have a sympathetic role model close to me. He helped my mother deal with her demons because he loved her. He was my father and my mother's chief advisor. He was the most loving and kind person I have ever known. He would often defend us to my mother, who would get angry very quickly and beat us unless he intervened. My father believed you can find reason and understanding through communication. He did not want his daughters to become just wives. He wanted us to be self-sufficient and educated. His belief was not traditional of most Hispanic fathers. He did not want his daughters to become victims of our culture. He shielded us and protected my sisters and I as best he could. I'm sure there were times when he over-protected us and times when he was too lenient. But his love, compassion and gentleness were the perfect ointments for our sociological wounds.

I am sure he had his critics—including my mom. I always felt that he believed society should honor its women more. I got the sense that he disagreed with women's second-class status. Times have changed—even in my little *barrio*—but, too many women remain oppressed.

Teen girls are a hot topic for magazines and talk shows. One of the most talked-about studies was conducted by the American Association of University Women in 1990. They surveyed 3,500 young people between the ages of nine and fifteen, and found that girls had a huge drop in their self-esteem during adolescence compared to their male counterparts. Girls are supposed to be princesses who live happily ever after with their Prince Charming; or secretaries, administrative assistants or nurses who play secondary roles in business, or CEO's of the home.

Girls are told they can do anything guys can do, like run for Congress, manage a business, anchor the evening news, become a military officer—but we also get the message that we had better look beautiful, thin and stylish while doing so. TV and magazine advertisers show successful women wearing the right cosmetics, the right clothing, the right hair style and the right high heeled shoes. Unbelievably, girls are still told that math and engineering are too tough for girls and we are chided for "throwing like a girl."

Boys have their challenges, too, in a society that compels them to be confrontational instead of nurturing, detached rather than communicative, macho instead of compassionate, and dominant instead of collaborative. Like their female counterparts boys have to deal with people's expectations of who they should be, how they should act and what they must become.

One thing is for certain—all of us have been "wounded" physically, emotionally and psychologically in

the process of growing up. Many of our cuts and scrapes have healed. Some have taken longer than others. Others have left life-long impressions. What all of this means is there are plenty of opportunities to help people who are suffering because there are many degrees of suffering.

When I think about suffering, I think about something Mother Teresa said:

> *It is very possible that you will find human beings very near to you, needing compassion and love. Do not deny them these. Show them above all, that you sincerely recognize that they are...Jesus Himself who is hidden under the guise of suffering.*

When you take these words to heart you can be nothing but compassionate and loving—and humble—when it comes to helping others. It is a reminder to me to allow my better qualities to surface regardless of the circumstances I face or the kind of people I must deal with on a day-to-day basis. I am fully aware that feeling compassion for someone who has wronged you or hurt you is hard to do. It doesn't mean you have to condone what they do or pretend it didn't happen. It simply means you must see their pain, acknowledge the damage they've done to themselves and to those around them, and offer as much sympathy and forgiveness as you can, or should, to ease their suffering.

I have found that there is a short leap from compassion to humility. Both qualities come from the heart and have love, goodwill and kindness as their foundations. Because humility is a quality that is so misunderstood, I want to give you my perspective. I learned a lot about humility as a child who grew up in a *barrio,* but I also learned about the power of servant leadership and executive humility as a Lt. Colonel. It's a quality that all truly great leaders have.

> Dear Colonel Kickbusch,
>
> Hearing you speak just made me feel so grateful for having such a great Mom who I know is always 100% behind me. My career dream is to become a pediatrician. I just love the thought of helping out all the little kids the most I can. To me, if I can help at least one person a day I feel great. I'm only 14, but my friends tell me that I'm way more wise than my age. If you could keep contact with me I would love to share my story about my dad with you. It must have taken so much determination to achieve your goals. I admire that so much. Well, I have to get ready to leave so I'm gonna have to end this. Hope you can read my writing. Keep doing what you are doing. You are a great inspiration.
>
> Sincerely,
> Javiel

Unfortunately, the word *humility* has negative connotations today. Most people associate this reverential human quality with a lack of self-assertiveness or confidence and lowered self-esteem. Some people believe a humble person has a martyr complex. They assume that person is willing to sacrifice his or her needs totally to help others. True humility, however, is knowing how to lift the emotional burdens of others by showing them the virtues of self-acceptance,

integrity and an understanding of one's place in the scheme of things.

People who practice humility believe that all things work together for good and that there is a divine plan for everything. They have a mature outlook on problems and disappointments. They make the most out of each day and accept the consequences of their actions.

I believe God is aware of our suffering and provides the help we need—if we allow it. I also believe no act of compassion, kindness or humility goes unnoticed. When you help someone else, God knows. When someone helps you, God notices. You've probably heard the expressions "what goes around comes around" and "what you sow, you reap." So, why not sow kindness and compassion in an humble way? You may not inherit a fortune like the servant in the story, but you will inherit something priceless. You'll inherit "jewels" like inner peace, personal satisfaction, dignity, a sense of rightness and completeness. You'll feel good about helping another human being, and you'll feel good about yourself.

Once while in New Orleans attending a week long Federally Employed Women Conference, I noticed a homeless woman on the same corner everyday. Everyone would wonder why she was there, but no one would approach her. I decided to introduce myself and she said her name was Molly. Molly asked "Are you not ashamed to talk to me?" I answered, "No, what would you like to do?" "I would like to have breakfast at the Marriott" she answered. The Marriott is where the conference was being held and they had put me up in the Presidential Suite so we proceeded to go in.

The bellman stopped us and questioned me about my guest. I told him that "we all deserve to be treated with respect" and I guess it touched him because he found us a table in a private dining area. When the waitress approached the table I introduced her to Molly and she said, "Yes, I've seen her outside many times" and respectfully told Molly she would be happy to serve her. It turns out that Molly was a pediatric nurse who had a nervous breakdown and could no longer work. She became homeless and was unable to receive medication because she had no address. She gave me the name of her brother in Washington D.C. As it happened, he was excited to hear from Molly. He said no one would help him find her because she was an adult. He waited her return home. Molly had saved the lives of many children, where were we when Molly needed us? So, when you see someone in need, remember you never know, they could be someone's daughter, mother, brother or son.

Reflection Exercises

1. The next time you meet someone (a classmate, teacher, parent, brother or sister, a store clerk, a postal service employee, bank teller, etc.) look into the person's eyes and give him or her a friendly smile, project a positive and confident attitude, and mentally bless the person. At the same time, don't be gushy. A simple "hello" or "how are you" will do.

   You will be amazed at how the other person will pick up on your warmth and "mental hospitality." This kind of greeting is especially helpful if someone needs encouragement, sympathy or advice. They will feel your compassion, kindness and radiant peacefulness (depending on your state of mind and emotional control) and have more confidence in themselves and in their ability to handle life's challenges.

   Keep a log or journal of your encounters. Record the types of people and the kind of help you provide. You may find a career emerge, or at the least, you will be able to dramatically improve your communication, coaching and human relations skills—all prerequisites for becoming a leader.

2. Offer yourself the same kind of compassion you give others. Stop judging yourself so harshly. Be kinder to yourself and eliminate any ill feelings you harbor toward yourself, especially for any mistakes you might have made. Become aware of how you treat yourself, the names you call yourself, and the way

you feel about yourself. At the end of each day for the next week, list the times you have shown compassion for what someone else is going through—include the times you've shown compassion toward yourself.

3. Practice a little humility. If someone tells you about their accomplishments or good fortune, just listen instead of adding your own achievements. If you get a chance, volunteer to carry someone's heavy knapsack or book bag. If your parents or a friend is tired, help them get settled on the couch or a chair and wait on them hand and foot for an hour or so. Take a few moments each day to appreciate your immediate surroundings, regardless of how grand or humble they might be. Help someone less fortunate than yourself. Thank God for your blessings. If you are confronted by mean-spirited and hurtful people, respond to their harshness or insults by seeing them as abrasive gifts. If you refuse the gift, whose gift is it? Spend some time caring for someone who is ill. Appoint yourself as their "servant" for a while.

Look beyond the obvious and see the bright light of goodness in everyone you meet.

Gratitude unlocks the fullness of life. It turns what we have into enough, and more. It turns denial into acceptance, chaos into order, confusion into clarity. It can turn a meal into a feast, a house into a home, a stranger into a friend. Gratitude makes sense of our past, brings peace for today, and creates a vision for tomorrow. *[Melody Beattie]*

All the goodness, beauty and gratefulness in a human being belongs to the one who knows how to express these qualities.

[Georgette LeBlanc]

If the only prayer you say your whole life is 'Thank you,' that would be enough.

[Meister Eckhart]

Chapter 4

Gratitude

A steady diet of "thanks-giving" can transform your life.

Giving thanks is a precondition for healthy, happy living. It is one of the chief ingredients for our maturation and growth. We need to give and receive a dose of it every day to fortify us from disappointments caused by ingratitude and self-centeredness. Unfortunately, we can't take a pill for ingratitude or a vaccination to protect us when people take us for granted or ignore us altogether. Thanksgiving is an attitude, and attitudes come from the core values that filter those attitudes.

In the musical, *The Man of La Mancha*, Don Quixote meets a street woman—a wild, wanton, street-wise wench named Aldonza. The man of La Mancha studies her for a moment and then announces that she is his lady. He calls

her Dulcinea. She mocks him with her laughter and assures him that she's no lady.

Despite her protests, Don Quixote sees something in her that she cannot see in herself. He tries to give her a glimpse of her true nature and urges her to believe in herself. He insists that she is a lady. She takes offense, believing he is trying to manipulate her. She spreads her arms defiantly, nearly exposing her breasts to show him the kind of woman she is. She screams that she is merely a kitchen maid and uses her anger to hide her hurt.

She is Aldonza the nobody, not Dulcinea the princess. She runs from the stage as the man from La Mancha whispers after her that she is his lady. At the close of the play, Don Quixote is dying. He feels his whole life has been for nothing. He considers himself a failure.

To his side comes Aldonza-Dulcinea who has become a lovely, cultured woman distinguished by her gentleness. Don Quixote does not recognize her at first, but then realizes she is his Dulcinea. She tells him he has saved her from a life of mediocrity and convinces him that his life has been worthwhile. He dies knowing the power of his influence.

As the story illustrates so powerfully, expressing your gratitude to someone can have a profound effect on him or her. An act of gratitude, you see, is like a piñata. When it breaks open, there are a lot of surprises inside—and all of the surprises are usually good. Once you get a piñata perspective, you have caught the essence of gratitude because gratefulness breaks barriers and showers everyone with good feelings. Thankfulness spreads sunshine into relationships.

The following account of a little girl's love and sensitivity for her Grandmother's predicament shows the

relationship between acts of kindness and gratitude. See if
you don't agree:

Once upon a time, there was a four-year-old girl named
Lucia. She loved her grandmother who was very old, wrin-
kled and white-haired. Her grandmother lived with Lucia
and her parents in a large house that sat on a hill.

Each day the sun peeped in the east windows, bathing
everything inside with warmth and light. Her grandmother's room was on the west side of the house which was
adjacent to a wooded lot. The sun never made it to her room.

One day Lucia asked her father, "Why doesn't the sun
want to peek into Grandma's room, too?

"It tries to, but the trees are too tall," replied her father.

"Then let's cut the trees down."

"We can't do that, darling, the trees belong to our neighbors."

"Well, then, let's turn our house around."

"Her mother overheard the conversation and came out of
the kitchen."

"Our house is much too heavy," said her mother.

"And it would cost too much to have a contractor move
it," added her amused father.

"Will Grandma ever have sunshine in her room?" asked
Lucia.

"Probably not, dearest, unless you can carry some to
her," said her sympathetic mother.

Lucia tried her best to think of a way to import sunshine
to her grandmother's room. She asked the Sun to shine
brighter. She prayed for help. She asked the trees to grow a
little slower and then recanted because she didn't want them
to stunt their growth.

She thought to herself, *I must take some sunshine to my Grandma.* "My Grandma loved the sun when she was little like me. I'm sure she loves it just as much now," she said aloud.

When she was eating breakfast one morning, she noticed that the sun was shining in her cup of hot chocolate. She placed her little hand over her cup and rushed to her grandmother's room.

"Look, Grandma. Look! I have some sunshine for you."

When she took her hand off the top of the cup, there was hot chocolate, but no sunshine.

She frowned and left her grandmother's room. Later that morning she noticed a ray of sunlight shining on top of one of the books her father had written.

She ran over to the book and planted her hand on the cover and raced into her grandmother's room.

"See, Grandma. Look. I've brought you some sun."

She lifted her hand, but the ray of sun had disappeared.

"Oh, I'm so sorry, Grandma. It was there a minute ago."

Her grandmother pulled her closer.

"The sun comes from your angelic face, my child," said her grandmother, "and it peeps out of your beautiful eyes. I don't need the outside sun when I have you."

Lucia did not understand how the sun could peep out of her eyes or radiate from her face. But she was glad to make her dear grandmother happy.

From that day on, whenever she ran into her grandmother's room, she would blink her eyes to show their brightness and watch the smile which came back at her from her grandmother who blinked back her own radiance.

Gratitude brings brightness to relationships. One of the quickest and most direct routes to improving relationships is to show people how much you appreciate them. Don't wait to show your appreciation for someone's sensitivity, artistic ability, musical talent, athletic prowess, work ethic or family values. Appreciate them now and avoid the rush! In the story above Lucia and her grandmother showed their mutual appreciation. They didn't wait for the "outside sun." They let their inner light shine.

One way to let your "sun" shine is through a journal—a gratitude journal. I'll describe the benefits of journaling in more detail in the Reflection Exercises at the end of this chapter. But for now I want to emphasize that a gratitude journal is a good way to remind you of all the things you have now instead of focusing on what you don't have. And I'm not just referring to material things like jewelry, cars, a big house or designer clothes.

Keeping a gratitude journal helps you develop an attitude of gratitude on a daily basis. For example, write down what a good breakfast you had this morning, how much you enjoyed your coffee or tea, the compliment you got about how nice you look, the five minutes driving time you saved going to work or school, the postcard you received from a vacationing friend, the extra ten dollars you discovered in your knapsack, the smile you got from an admirer. List all of the good things that happen to you during the course of a normal day.

I feel I must explain one thing about gratitude and thanksgiving before you read further. I'd like you to know the difference between being grateful for something and being grateful in all things. I don't believe anyone has to be grateful for things like an illness, abusive childhood, drug addiction, losing a job, being betrayed by a friend, or going

through a divorce. But I do believe you need to keep an attitude of gratefulness in the midst of fighting an illness,
dealing with child abuse, battling drug addiction, losing a
job or dealing with a friend's betrayal. The gratefulness I'm
referring to is a thankfulness of the lessons learned from the
experience.

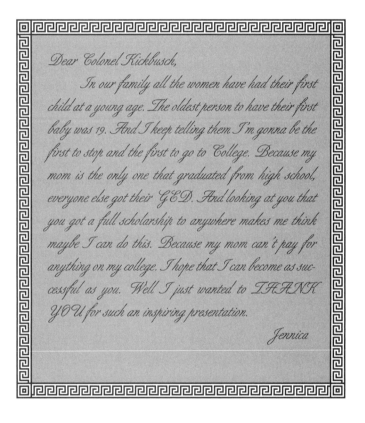

Dear Colonel Kickbusch,

In our family all the women have had their first child at a young age. The oldest person to have their first baby was 19. And I keep telling them I'm gonna be the first to stop and the first to go to College. Because my mom is the only one that graduated from high school, everyone else got their GED. And looking at you that you got a full scholarship to anywhere makes me think maybe I can do this. Because my mom can't pay for anything on my college. I hope that I can become as successful as you. Well I just wanted to THANK YOU for such an inspiring presentation.

Jennica

As a *barrio* "graduate" (I could also say *barrio* "sur-
vivor") I am not thankful for my *barrio* experience as much
as I am grateful for the lessons that environment taught me.
I may have lived in a *barrio*, but I've never been from the

barrio as far as it means to deserve to come from one. At one time it was my physical address, but it has never been my "permanent" address. I come from a higher place– and so do you! I may have come through a *barrio* to become what I am today, but I came from a loving family who wanted me to succeed, no matter how humble my beginnings.

I have one more thing to say about gratitude journalizing before we move on. I suggest this tool because it helps us shift our attitudes to a "consciousness of thanksgiving" and brings positive thinking to our hearts. When you develop an attitude of gratitude and begin to appreciate your blessings—no matter how small—you have succeeded in a journey that many kids never attempt. Gratitude is a major signpost, or should I say milepost, along your roadmap toward success. And your gratitude journal is your trip ticket.

Sarah Ban Breathnach in her best-selling book, *Simple Abundance: A Daybook of Comfort and Joy,* sums up what I've just said. She writes:

> *The gratitude journal has to be a necessary step on your path or it just won't work for you. Simplicity, order, harmony, beauty, prayer and joy—all the other principles that can transform your life will not blossom and flourish without gratitude. If you want to successfully travel this journey, use a gratitude journal. Why? Because you simply will not be the same person two months from now after consciously giving thanks each day for the blessings that exist in your life. And you will have set in motion an ancient spiritual law; the more you have and are grateful for, the more will be given you.*

Gratitude

The best advice I can give you is to keep a gratitude journal and prove it to yourself. I can tell you from personal experience that once you begin thinking thankfully, you will begin to act thankfully and feel thankfully. You will develop a positive way of looking at things which will help you handle situations much more confidently and faithfully.

People who are unappreciative tend to complain about life. They cultivate negative attitudes. Constant dissatisfaction and ungratefulness lower our energy levels and cause us to carry our fatigue around with us like a shadow. One of the most hurtful reactions we can have to anyone's kindness is ingratitude. Ungratefulness is a costly mistake in any relationship, so I urge you to cultivate a thankful heart and a willingness to appreciate what others do for you.

In recent years, advances in social science have helped to explain our collective understanding of what leads to our health, happiness, vitality and longevity. Our current understanding is that the people who are most likely to survive and thrive are the ones who adapt and express many of the core values outlined in this book. Is it any wonder I want to pass them on to you? I want you to survive. I want you to succeed. I want you to serve!

This brings to mind the image of a bridge that spans a great canyon. The heavier load the bridge must bear, the more supportive elements are required to keep it from collapsing under the weight. The same thing applies to us. As each of us struggles to manage the heavy load of pressures and stresses we must bear, those of us who offer support and who are supported by others stand a much better chance of holding up rather than caving in to the pressures life throws at us.

Being grateful for that kind of support is an important life skill to develop because it means our chances of sur-

vival—and success—are greater. It improves our chances because people tend to help people who appreciate their help. A simple "thank you" goes a long way.

I am coming to believe that gratitude is a courageous act. It is an admission that we need other people, that we can't do it alone. It shows we recognize how miracles occur through the acts of regular people. I believe that whenever we thank a human being for helping us, we are thanking the Universe for putting that person there to provide that help.

Reflection Exercises

1. The words, "Think and Thank" are inscribed in many churches throughout Europe. Come to think of it, these words should be inscribed in our hearts and minds, too. We would have a better chance of becoming the success we'd like to be if we would think before we speak and offer thanks for the blessings we receive daily. Think of ten things you have taken for granted this past week. (For example, your mother cooked all of your meals, you are wearing the clothes your parents bought you, your brother or sister took out the trash you were supposed to take out, it didn't rain so you didn't have to mow the grass, you got an "A" on a test at school). List each of them below:

    When you have completed your list, approach each one of the people who helped you and thank him or her face-to-face, in writing or an email. Compile a gratitude list for next week and repeat the process.

2. When you feel especially thankful this week bring you palms together, lower yourself to your knees, and give thanks for your blessings. I call this sending knee-mail. Let your gratitude trail off into silence for a few moments before you rise.

3. Become aware of when you wish you were somewhere else this week or doing something different. Bring yourself back to a state of appreciation for where you are and who you are. Not appreciating where you are at the moment is nothing more than a habit that you have the option of breaking right now.

4. Make a list of 101 things you are thankful for in your life. Think of as many as you can in one sitting. If you can't think of 101 things at one sitting, promise yourself you will.

    Complete the list in a day or two. Read back over your list and think about each item. Try to remember the people involved, the place, when the event happened, how you felt about it and how it has changed your life. Keep this list handy and pull it out the next time you need a motivational lift.

Gratitude is the ticket to admission for more blessings.

Honesty is the cornerstone of all success.
[Mary Kay Ash]

Integrity implies that we become all that we are it implies a conscious, purposeful way of acting. It involves a total commitment to who and what we are.
[Ann Hillman]

When we are honest with ourselves, we must admit our lives are all that really belong to us. So it is how we use our lives that determines the kind of people we become.
[Cesar Chavez]

Chapter 5

Honesty and Integrity

Where we stand depends on what we fall for.

Once a high school principal decided to test the honesty of his teachers, so he invited them into his study and posed the following question:

"What would you do if you were walking along and found a wallet full of money lying on the road?"

The principal waited for the group to respond.

"I'd return it to its owner immediately," exclaimed one teacher.

His answer comes much too quickly. I wonder if he means it, the principal thought to himself.

"I'd keep the money and donate it to charity," said another.

He certainly seems philanthropic. I wonder whose char-ity, the principal thought to himself.

"To be honest, boss," replied the third teacher, "I believe I'd be tempted to keep it, but I'd pray for the strength to resist the temptation. Then I hope I'd do the right thing and return it."

Ahh, thought the principal. Here is an employee I can trust.

As you can tell I like using stories to illustrate important points. In the above story the princi-pal knew the difference between people who parrot what they think you want to hear and someone who speaks from the heart. You probably know people who fit those two cat-egories. The thing to remember is: *where you stand depends on what you'll fall for.* And I can tell you without one ounce of doubt that standing on honesty and integrity is standing on solid ground.

Webster's *American College Dictionary* defines honesty as "the ability to be truthful, just, sincere and fair instead of false and misleading." The definition given for integrity is "uprightness of character; being true to one's values and beliefs; a refusal to engage in fraud or deceit." These descriptions of honesty and integrity are textbook defini-tions, but they remind us that these two character traits are more than words on paper. They are choices that define us and our actions.

If we think about our actions ahead of time and then follow through on those actions based on our beliefs and

values, chances are we will do the right thing to begin with because we've stood on our principles. The advantage of acting out of honesty and integrity is that we won't have to pay the consequences for poor choices later. Honesty and integrity generally keep us out of trouble, and they are both personal qualities that help build our reputations.

Each day we meet people we enter into a social contract where information, attitudes and impressions are exchanged. The more interactions we experience, the more we learn about people and the more they learn about us. In time we develop a reputation. When it comes to our thoughts, words and actions, we can tell the truth and keep our promises and commitments or misrepresent ourselves by becoming dishonest and undependable. The choice is ours.

❖ If we remain true to our beliefs and values we
   will find that people will learn:
❖ they can trust us
❖ we are dependable
❖ we are responsible for our actions
❖ to believe what we say
❖ to rely on us
❖ we honor our word

In other words, we will earn a good reputation, and that reputation will bring us strong relationships, important social and business alliances, and a great deal of satisfaction and inner peace. People—whether they are our family, friends, school mates, teachers, counselors or business people—would rather deal with an honest person than someone they can't trust. That is a fact of life.

Think about your own circle of friends or people you have dealt with outside of the family or school. Who do you

trust? Is there someone you wouldn't trust? Do you know someone who is undependable or irresponsible? Does someone distrust you for any reason? What kind of reputation do you have? How many people would say you have integrity?

I can say this without any hesitation—once you have been untruthful, undependable and untrustworthy even once, people's trust in you falters. If you disappoint them a second, or third time, they lose their trust in you altogether.

Being honest all of the time isn't easy. It takes discipline to protect your reputation. For example, being honest requires you to be tactful and diplomatic at all times as well as being truthful. Sometimes it means you have to tell people what they may not want to hear. It even forces you to admit to things you'd rather not divulge. Occasionally, your honesty may even upset friends who think you are being too honest.

When students ask me what they should do about their honesty, especially when they know the truth will upset someone, I tell them it is better to experience the awkward truth now than become victimized by a lie later. Camryn Manheim, the Emmy Award-winning actress from the popular TV show, *The Practice,* includes a quiz about honesty in her book, *Wake Up, I'm Fat!* One of the questions she asks is: "Do you tell yourself the truth…or do you lie to yourself?

She makes a good point. Do you tell yourself "I am an honest person," and then tell a lie later that day? Do you say, "I take good care of my body," and then abuse it by taking drugs or drinking alcohol? Have you ever said, "I value education," and then skipped school for a couple of days?

Are you honest with yourself about honoring your relationship with friends, sticking to your diet and exercise

regime, keeping your word, assessing your future, setting goals, maintaining a mature outlook on life? When you borrow money, do you repay the lender in a reasonable amount of time? When you are debating where to go and what to do with your friends, do they know where you stand on key issues? Do you voice your opinion even when you know you may be ridiculed or left out of a group activity? Do you pretend to be something you are not and expect people to believe you?

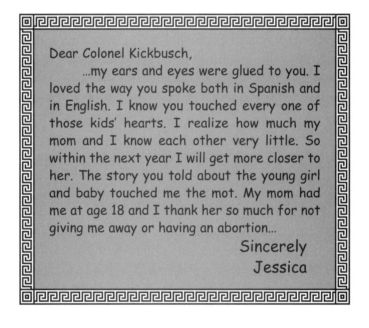

Dear Colonel Kickbusch,
   ...my ears and eyes were glued to you. I loved the way you spoke both in Spanish and in English. I know you touched every one of those kids' hearts. I realize how much my mom and I know each other very little. So within the next year I will get more closer to her. The story you told about the young girl and baby touched me the mot. My mom had me at age 18 and I thank her so much for not giving me away or having an abortion...

Sincerely
Jessica

Here is a true story of two people who misrepresented themselves by being dishonest:

Rob Pilatus and Fabrice Morvan were handsome, muscular and talented musicians. They loved to dance and entertain their audiences with stunning routines. They sold millions of singles and albums and won a Grammy in Jan-

uary of 1990 for Best New Artists. Milli Vanilli was at the top of the music world. They were HOT!

During one of their engagements, something happened to the sound equipment. The tape which held all of their vocal arrangements broke. Milli Vanilli could not continue singing **because it was not their voices on the tape.** The vocal sounds their audiences adored were actually studio artists Brad Howell and John Davis. Rob Pilatus and Fabrice Morvan had been lip-syncing all along. They had faked singing every song.

In case you are wondering, other singing groups tape their own voices when they have to sing and dance as part of their routine. However, in the case of Milli Vanilli, two other singers were doing the singing while Pilatus and Morvan got all of the recognition, credit and profit.

When the incident was investigated further, authorities found that Pilatus and Morvan were such terrible vocalists that their manager and producer refused to let them expose their less than cultured voices. He suggested that they stick to instrumental sounds. They fired him. Shortly after that, the sound failure exposed how they were duping the public. And for the first time in Grammy history, the prestigious award was withdrawn.

How could two talented musicians have gotten themselves into such a mess? Time Magazine reported, "They were living a marginal life in a Munich housing project when, in 1988, Farian (the producer) offered each of them $4,000 (plus royalties) to be seen but not heard as Milli Vanilli."

After the scandal, they tried to make a comeback, but never quite regained their audience or their reputation. VH1's Behind the Music broadcast a biography on the rise

and fall of Milli Vanilli. In 1998, Rob Pilatus died at the age of thirty-two of an apparent drug-alcohol cocktail overdose in Frankfurt, Germany. Former Milli Vanilli partner Fabrice Morvan was quoted in E!Online News as saying: "I'm feeling tremendous pain and sorrow upon hearing the news of my friend and brother, Rob. He will always be a part of me. We struggled together and succeeded together. All we ever wanted to do was perform."

It wasn't their aspirations that caused their demise. Milli Vanilli chose to be dishonest and pretend to be something they were not. Unfortunately, all of the "success," recognition and money they got were based on a lie—which turned out to be a career stopper.

Dishonesty can be a relationship's stopper, too! It can spoil friendships and family closeness. The negative effects of deceit can sour peoples' opinions of the deceiver and ruin reputations. Once dishonesty has left its stamp on a relationship—any kind of relationship—the road to regain the trust, respect and credibility that have been lost is a long one. Sometimes trust is never restored.

One comment I hear much too often when I speak at schools is: "Everyone lies and it's no big deal unless someone gets hurt." Another unsettling comment is: "Lying is not a crime, unless you're caught. Look at what happened at Enron and Arthur Anderson. They were lying for years before they got caught. Everybody knew about it, but nobody did anything about it until it was too late."

I understand these students' sentiments, but unscrupulous means do not justify profitable ends. They never will!

84

It is unfortunate that dishonest people "get away" with their deceitfulness sometimes. But I believe they pay an emotional, physical and spiritual price every time they misrepresent the truth. I also believe, sooner or later, they reap what they sow.

Dishonesty can get you a lot of things: an A on a test, but not a good night's sleep; a date, but not a lasting relationship; praise, but not respect; out of immediate trouble, but not peace of mind; sympathy, but not self-esteem; out of a previous lie, but not out of a poor reputation.

I encourage you to live a life full of honesty and integrity because a reputation is all you have. A good reputation is like a flower. In order for the flower to grow properly and thrive, it must be "fed" and watered, given the right amount of light and repotted or replanted at the proper time. The same holds true for your reputation. Nurturing your reputation with honesty and integrity is a daily requirement. Feeding it with truthfulness, sincerity and authenticity will cause your reputation to grow as a towering testament to your strength of character.

Reflection Exercises

1. Test your honesty and integrity. Give honest answers by completing each of the following statements:

   I'm perfectly satisfied with…

   I find I can no longer …

   I regret that I haven't …

   I'm finally at peace with …

   The thing I wish I had done more of is …

   For me, drugs and alcohol are …

   The best advice I can give to classmates is …

   The thing I need to change most about myself is …

   I'm most proud of myself when I …

   Whenever I hear hurtful gossip about someone, I…

   I wish my parent/foster parent/mother/father would …

   I wish I could …

   Looking back on my life, I've learned that …

2. Give your interpretation of the following quote attributed to George C. Lichtenberg: "The most dangerous of all falsehoods is a slightly distorted truth."

3. List five things you would like to be more honest about when it comes to hanging out with your friends.

4. If you are honest enough to admit it, what one thing would you like to change about yourself that might alienate you from your current pack of friends—or if you are a loner, might attract more friends than you are used to?

5. What do you really want to be when you grow up?

Look into people as well as at them.

Confidence is courage at ease.

[Daniel Maher]

Bedazzled by the dizzying complexity and breakneck pace of our modern lives, our wobbly [confidence] has exiled us from the vitality of staying in touch with the deep core of our wholeness.   [Michelle Levey]

Motivation will almost always beat mere talent.

[Normal Augustine]

Chapter 6

Motivation and Confidence

People who succeed have more will power than won't power.

Jennifer Lindsay, a twenty-one year old violin virtuoso and 1999 Essence Magazine Award winner, suffered a severe loss of oxygen when she was born that left her brain-damaged. Doctors told her mother that Jennifer would never be normal and that she was a likely candidate for institutionalization. The doctors didn't realize that her mother had more will power than won't power—and that little Jennifer had inherited the same gene.

Her mother quit her job as a junior high school teacher to devote all of her time to taking care of her daughter. By age three Jennifer was reading at a second grade level. At five, she was playing the violin extremely well, so well in fact, that she was considered gifted. At thirteen, Jennifer was

excelling in college courses and at sixteen scored 1560 out of 1600 on her SAT (Scholastic Aptitude Test).

What if her mother had believed the doctor's initial prognosis? Suppose she had felt so sorry for her predicament and her daughter's disability that she had given up before she started? Imagine if she had not devoted herself to her daughter's growth and development during those first few critical years? What if she had not taken Jennifer to special doctors and childhood development experts? What if she had not home-schooled Jennifer with the loving care of someone who saw tremendous potential in a young girl with a disability? Suppose she had neglected to motivate her daughter to become all she could be—in spite of the complications at her birth?

Jennifer's story doesn't end there. She tutors music students, and she gives musical performances at churches, assisted living homes, private clubs and organizations. She is a confident and motivated young woman—and the product of the love, daring and indomitable spirit of a proud mother. Her story shows us what we can do if someone believes in us enough to help us see our own potential. The confidence Jennifer's mother had in her daughter's ability must have rubbed off, and so did her generosity and perseverance and kindness. Jennifer was transformed by her mother's belief in her daughter's worth as a human being. She believed her daughter had a rightful place in the world and would not accept anything less than a happy, healthy, productive youngster that would grow into a capable woman.

Jennifer's story reminds me of a well-known musical that had its beginnings in Greek mythology. You may have studied it in school, but it is worth repeating here because it fits so nicely with Jennifer's story.

Pygmalion, the King of Cyprus, was a great sculptor. One day, he carved a statue of a beautiful young woman purely out of his imagination. No woman had modeled her, no woman could compare. The young king fell in love with his own creation and was so smitten that he spent all his time gazing at her and thinking about her.

He wished she was a real flesh and blood woman, but knew she was crafted from ivory. Lovesick, the yearning Pygmalion summoned Aphrodite the goddess of beauty, love and fertility. He pleaded with her to bring his beautiful statue to live. Although she was reluctant to do so, Aphrodite granted the bewitched king his wish and gave the statue life.

Based on this classic tale, playwright George Bernard Shaw wrote *Pygmalion* for the theatre. You may remember it as the delightfully spun musical *My Fair Lady*. In the stage version, Professor Henry Higgins teaches phonetics and meets the perfect person to test his specialty, an ill-spoken Cockney flower girl named Eliza Doolittle.

Higgins believes, by the force of his immense skill and will he can transform the poor flower girl into a striking lady. Like the King of Cyprus, his efforts are successful and he manages to transform the reluctant flower girl into a radiant lady. To add to his excitement, Eliza begins to believe in herself. She becomes a lady on the inside as well as she appears to be in her dress and demeanor.

Psychologists, sociologists and behavioral scientists have long known the benefits of expectancy and conditioning. Robert K. Merton, a sociology professor at Columbia University was the first researcher to coin the phrase "self-fulfilling prophecy." He theorized that when an influential person expects another person to behave in a certain way, that person's behavior tends to meet those expectations.

Harvard Psychologist, Robert Rosenthal, expanded Merton's self-fulfilling prophecy notion and called it the "Pygmalion Effect" in honor of the mythical King of Cyprus. His research team proved that people tend to live up—or down—to our expectations of them. They also discovered that when people learn they are capable of performing according to expectations, they begin to develop confidence in themselves, which reinforces their newfound competencies. The more they meet expectations—positive or negative—the more self-reinforcing their successes.

Although we can't turn an ivory statue into a real person, we can like Jennifer's mother, transform people's static view of themselves so they can discover and then honor talents, skills and abilities they didn't know they possessed. The more confidence we show someone we have in his or her ability, the more confident he or she tends to be.

Lack of confidence robs us of a tremendous number of opportunities to showcase our talents and growth. It puts a damper on our achievements and blocks our creativity. If you are in the "army" of teens who lack confidence in yourself, this chapter has been written for you and is dedicated toward your becoming a more charismatic, confident person.

My objective for this chapter is to show you how to gain the confidence that lies dormant within you and use it to boost the level of satisfaction you feel about your ability

to do anything you set your mind to do. All of us have felt unsure of ourselves from time to time. But it is important to be who we are. Charles Schultz did a masterful job of capturing those feelings using his famous cartoon character, Charlie Brown.

Charlie Brown, Linus and Lucy are lying on a hillside one afternoon looking up at the clouds.

Lucy says, "If you use your imagination you can see a lot of things in cloud formations. What do you see, Linus?"

"Well those clouds up there look like the map of British Honduras on the Caribbean. That big cloud over there looks a little like the profile of Thomas Eakins, the famous sculptor and painter. And that cluster of clouds to our left gives me the impression of the stoning of Stephen. I can see the Apostle Paul standing there to one side."

"Uh huh…that's very good. What do you see in the clouds, Charlie Brown?" Lucy asks.

Charlie Brown responds in his typically shy manner, "Well I was going to say I saw a ducky and a horsie, but I've changed my mind."

There is a lot of truth in this humorous story. So often we hide our true thoughts and feelings because we are afraid of criticism and alienation from people or groups we want to be a part of. Actor Hector Elizondo shares a childhood sorry about his journey from a weak, scared, sickly kid to a position of courage and confidence. He explains:

I didn't want to be scared anymore so I used my own initiative. I overcome my fears and literally reinvented myself physically—totally—by working and getting stronger. I lacked confidence, so I knew I had to become more confident...A very rambunctious fighting group of boys had singled me out to pick on...After the fourteenth time of being humiliated, I fought back—and won the fight! I learned that you have to be brave and that sometimes someone or something motivates you to be brave.

Self-confidence is like a muscle. It needs to be strengthened and given a workout every day. Otherwise, we tend to manufacture reasons why we cannot do something or invent excuses to hide our lack of confidence in ourselves. People who lack self-confidence usually see things that aren't there and convince themselves that they lack the skills and knowledge to be successful.

Dear Colonel Kickbusch,
Thank you for everything you taught me. You really inspired me to try to achieve big things. I thank you so much for that.

Sincerely,
Michael

P.S. When I make it big and you see me on television I want you to know some of that success came from your speech. Have a nice day. Write back if you ever get time.

I'd like to share another quick story. It involves a frightened lab psychologist, and shows what happens when our lack of confidence leads to false assumptions. It appears in William Haney's thoroughly interesting book, *Communication and Interpersonal Relations*.

According to Haney, a psychologist had been keeping his experimental white mice in the attic of his university's psychology building. One afternoon, the psychologist discovered that several of the mice had gotten out of their cages. Some of them were dead and partly eaten. He immediately recalled that several months earlier, a couple of students had reported seeing wild rats in the building. They had set traps, but were not successful in catching anything.

Realizing the danger the wild rats represented, the psychologist raced downstairs to retrieve a tennis racket he had noticed earlier. When he returned to the attic, tennis racket-weapon in hand, he saw to his dismay a wild gray rat sitting directly in front of one of the cages. The rat appeared to be trembling. The psychologist took a few cautious steps toward the rodent to improve his aim, and then hurled the tennis racket at the defiant rat. When the rat did not move, the psychologist became angry and threw a book at the bold creature. (What an awful way to treat a book, don't you think?) When the rat still didn't budge, the infuriated psychologist stamped his feet, flung his arms and made all of the noise he could as he charged the rat—only to discover that the "rat" was a crumpled piece of gray paper.

His prior belief about the existence of wild rats running amok contributed to his assumption that the harmless gray piece of paper was a cannibalistic rat. He had initially expected to see healthy, caged white mice. When he encountered the dead mice outside their cage, he naturally assumed they were killed and eaten by their wild gray cousins. He assumed that the crumpled gray paper must be one of those renegade wild rats.

In this humorous example of self-deception lies one of the most fascinating and perhaps awesome aspects of human nature: We see what we expect to see, and what we expect to see is what the rational mind does to eliminate or reduce ambiguity and uncertainty. To make some kind of sense out of our experience, we seek immediate closure to our problems, even if that closure is delusional.

Because we are literally bombarded with stimuli, our five senses automatically choose what to pay attention to and we base our assumptions on what we interpret from those five senses. In human behavioral terms, the eye can handle approximately five million bits of information per second. Isn't that amazing? So some type of selection is inevitable because we see what we want to in order to protect our own view of the world. People who lack motivation or self-confidence tend to see barriers and reasons why they can't do something. Like the lab psychologist, they assume the worst.

Every time we attempt to do something new or challenging, it involves risk and moving out of our comfort zone—sometimes way out of our comfort zone. Entering new situations, meeting people we don't know, facing a tough obstacle are all things that test our self-confidence. But they also teach us! We learn our abilities and our limits, our likes and dislikes, our strengths and our weaknesses.

Everyone to some degree or another suffers from a lack of confidence. Nobody is perfect and no one has a monopoly on courage. Believe it or not, I still get quite scared to stand in front of an audience and deliver a keynote address. I call this fear my personal demons at work. The key to gaining more self-confidence is to recognize what you do well and take advantage of your talents by staying positive, affirming how special you are, and adapting life-enriching attitudes that amplify your strengths.

What images, feelings, thoughts or memories come to your mind when you read this word: *scared*? It means frightened, afraid, terrified and panicked, right? Now what if you saw the word: *sacred*? It means holy, blessed, heavenly and exalted, right?

These words have entirely different meanings and yet they have every letter in common. The only difference is that the "a" and the "c" are transposed. But what a difference that is! I believe that by making a tiny shift in your thinking, you cannot only transform a scared moment into a sacred one, but you can transform your *lack* of confidence into the *luck* of confidence.

Henry David Thoreau, the well-known American writer, offered excellent advice on the subject of self-confidence, no matter what our fears and doubts might tell us. He said that if we advance confidently in the direction of our dreams, and try to live the kind of life that makes us happy and fulfilled, we will begin to have unimaginable success. I agree with this assertion because I have witnessed thousands of young people move from lack of confidence past their doubts and become successful in the area they have chosen. I can also promise you that if a young girl, raised in a *barrio* called *El Rincon del Diablo* (The Devil's Den) can succeed despite the odds, you can too!

I don't want to sound harsh, but I have very little toler-ance for the attitude—"I can't get anywhere because of where I live." Toney Anaya grew up in a one-bedroom adobe in northern New Mexico. He became Governor of New Mexico. The film *Stand and Deliver* was based on the inspiring teacher Jaime Escalante, who motivated students at Garfield-Roosevelt High School in the *barrio* of East Los Angeles to excel at an unbelievable level of performance. Actor Anthony Quinn grew up in a "small hut on a knoll on a plantation," as he tells it. None of these people used where they lived as an excuse to fail.

I remember one high school counselor who laughed at me when I showed interest in going to college. The coun-selor told me that all of the girls from my "side of town" were good for one thing and one thing only—making babies! I remember being embarrassed and angry. My father encouraged me to get a second, third or fourth opinion if I had to, but to persevere. I followed his sage-like advice and decided that I was college material—and that someday, when I met the right man, I would marry and have those children the insensitive counselor predicted I would have. I am proud to say I have five daughters— and two college degrees. The counselor's rudeness and insensitivity moti-vated me to ask myself what I really wanted out of life. I learned that no one knows enough about your potential and abilities to say you can't succeed in a given area of interest. The *only* person who can determine that is *you*. I decided never to let anyone, anything or any experience determine the quality of my life.

Eleanor Roosevelt once said "no one can intimidate you without your consent." I believe no one can motivate you without your consent, too! So, I encourage you to con-sent to the incredible edge you have over everybody else

just by being you. No one else can ever be exactly like you. They may have similar talents and skills, but they will never have your potential.

The good news is you don't have to be the brightest person in the world, but you do have to be eager and persistent. In fact, my first college entrance exam revealed that I was borderline retarded! What that test did not measure was my true abilities. You have to decide that you will become someone who is destined to succeed, no matter what. You must develop a quality of pushing ahead when the criticism is toxic and the going is tough. You can succeed by working harder and more confidently one step, one positive thought, one choice at a time.

Reflection Exercises

1. Pick a theme word or phrase for a week or a month. Use words or phrases like: success, happiness, staying positive, excel, living confidently, practicing humility, honesty, being grateful, showing respect, etc. Spend 5 to 15 minutes at the end of each day thinking about how you experienced the theme word or phrase. Record your thoughts in a journal or notebook.

2. On a 3 x 5 index card or similar piece of paper, write one adjective describing how you want tomorrow to be. Use positive, life-affirming adjectives like:

amusing	non-threatening
artistic	nutritious
beneficial	peaceful
creative	productive
decision-making	rejuvenating
enriching	restful
fulfilling	rewarding
fun-filled	spectacular
happy	successful
joyful	volunteering

3. As you consider who you would like to become, what career you would enjoy and what life you would like to live, complete the following statements:

I see myself as a person who:

I see myself enjoying a career in:
because:

The thing that motivates me the most is:

I am aware that I need to develop confidence in my ability to:

I am aware I need to eliminate:

If I could do those last two things above, I would be:

A person I know who fits this image is:

Transform your "lack" of
confidence into the
"luck" of confidence.

My father instilled in me,   Respect yourself, get your education and career together, and then if you happen to meet a great guy, you'll meet him on the right level.

Sandra Bullock]

Lack of respect is the most basic crime of all because it covers most other crimes.

[Edward de Bono]

The respect for the rights of others is peace.

[Benito Juarez]

Chapter 7

Respect

Respect is not bought, it must be earned.
El respeto no se compra—se tiene que merecer.

Earl Loomis in *The Self In Pilgrimage* tells the story of a little boy who joined his mother and older sister for lunch. After taking the mother's and sister's orders, the waitress addressed the youngster.

"What will you have, young man?"

"I'll order for him," emphasized his mother, who steeled her gaze on the waitress.

Undaunted, the waitress re-addressed the youngster, "Young man, what will you have today?"

"A cheeseburger," the lad whispered.

"Would you like it medium or well done?"

"Well done, please," said the youngster, brightening a bit.

"Would you like mustard, pickles, onions, relish or ketchup?"

In a burst of self-confidence, the boy exclaimed, "The whole works! I want everything."

As the waitress walked away, the lad looked happily at his chaperones.

"Gee, Mom, she thinks I'm a real person."

espect, as defined in Webster's dictionary, is "to esteem...to honor." To esteem is to set a value on or to rate highly. Now that we know the formal definition of respect we need to ask, do we respect ourselves? Sometimes we respect ourselves the least of all the people with whom we interact. If we respect ourselves, we will not put ourselves in danger. If we respect our bodies we will not place our bodies in situations that will cause us discomfort or pain. If we respect our inner selves—our emotional state—we will not jeopardize our emotional well-being by becoming involved in unhealthy relationships or adopt self-defeating behaviors.

Yet how many of us go against the respect we should have for ourselves? We ingest pills or drugs that enhance our moods in order to "feel better," only to find we feel worse afterward. We allow that little pill, that cigarette, that injection, that drug that is supposed to elevate our mood, to conquer us. We disrespect ourselves every time we engage in those activities.

Respect

What about the danger we place our bodies in when we engage in promiscuous sexual activity? What are we exposing ourselves to? Most of you know the answer—we choose many ways to disrespect our body. Among them are sexually transmitted diseases (which can cause damage to unborn babies, infertility, and mental and physical degeneration in later life), and AIDS. We know the answers, yet we are in denial when we expect that our irresponsible behavior will not put us at risk. Every year approximately 3 million American teenagers contract a sexually transmitted disease (STD). STD's facilitate the transmission of HIV. According to a recent White House Report on Youth and HIV/AIDS, approximately half of all new HIV infections each year occur among people age 25 and younger. Public Health officials believe that 20,000 people between the ages of 13 and 24 are infected every year—that translates to an infection rate of 2 people per hour.

What emotional traumas do we place our emotional health in when we get involved in abusive, negative relationships? These relationships breed fear, anger, conflict and stress. If our emotional health is not in good order, our physical well being is compromised as well. If we are not thinking clearly, we cannot concentrate in school or at work. We jeopardize our success by focusing on situations outside our control.

For example, let's look at the young woman who really loves her boyfriend. She tells him this repeatedly, yet he says he cannot believe she truly loves him unless she "proves" her love by having sex with him. She is not ready for sex and does not want to indulge in this behavior. Yet, she is torn between her love for her boyfriend, the values her parents have taught her, her growing sexual awareness and curiosity, and her respect for herself—her body. With

this "parade of confusion" in her head she can no longer concentrate on her school studies. She feels sick inside. So, she compromises herself and gives in to her boyfriend's demands.

Unfortunately, she has set herself up for another set of problems. Now she feels guilty. While she loves her boyfriend, she may also resent him now for pushing her into something for which she was not ready. Now she may worry about being pregnant—and then she will really get sick! She has lost more than she expected to gain—she has lost her self-respect. It's obvious she doesn't know the facts. For example, one of every ten teen fathers never raise their children. They are absentee fathers. Every 29 seconds a young woman under the age of 15 delivers a baby. Here's another sobering fact for you: It will cost a parent $164,000 to feed, clothe, educate and provide room and board for a child from birth to 18 years.

Sexual intimacy is not just something that happens without any thought given to showing respect for the other person, or communicating about using protection, getting pregnant, or catching sexually-transmitted diseases (STD's). In the fantasy world created by TV and movie producers, love scenes are usually erotic, passionate and spontaneous acts of lust and abandon. The following example is based on a scene from a popular TV series:

> *Cindy and Chris work together. They have flirted with each other, but never kissed. One night Chris arrives at Cindy's house and climbs the trellis to her window, waking her up. Cindy comes to the window in her bathrobe.*
>
> *Chris: "Cindy. I know it's late, but I have something I want to ask you."*

Cindy: *"Shhh! Try to be quiet or you'll wake my parents."*

Chris: *"Oops, I'm sorry. I love you, Cindy. Life is not the same without you. Please let me come in."*

Cindy steps back to allow Chris enough room to climb in to her bedroom. Seductive music begins. She pulls off her robe, revealing a silky nightgown. He pulls off his shirt and they begin to kiss. He caresses her hair and runs his hand down her face and arm. They continue kissing as he lowers both of them onto her bed. Lights fade. The music fades. Break for commercial.

What's missing from this scene? They obviously were becoming quite intimate. Did they have sex? We're supposed to think so. Did they discuss precautions? Birth control? Protection? Morals? Self-respect? Not according to the choreographed scene. Oftentimes, young people have a soap opera or TV series impression of intimacy that turns romance into a warped reality.

I will never forget the story of a young lady in high school who discovered she got pregnant by a young man over a $20 bet. One day in gym class, a group of guys dared a friend to "do it" with a young, quiet girl whom guys believed was a "hard nut to crack." One guy, finding himself all caught up in the testosterone hype, responded, "It will take time, but I will be collecting."

He carried her books and spoke nicely to her. He waited for her after class and after school. He gained her trust and confidence. He had a plan for his naive companion: She was slowly being wooed and set up to fall in love.

Towards the end of the school year, he "scored" and "scored big," according to him. He got her to lie to her parents and had set up a place to seduce her and have sex. She eventually gave up her body over a measly $20 bet! She was what many young men described as "a girl so nice and naive, it's really no challenge at all!" A few months later, she discovered her menstruation had stopped and she was pregnant.

She immediately met him in school and told him, "I'm pregnant! What are we going to do?" He replied, "This is your baby, not mine! Besides, I just won $20 from the guys who dared me to have sex with you." To which he added, "Do you think I believe I am the only guy who's had sex with you? You gave it to me so easily—what makes you think I believe you were a virgin?"

Do you think he respected her? Definitely not. He didn't respect himself, either. No self-respecting young adult would treat another human being like that.

The young woman left crying hysterically and eventually told her mother the truth. In the following months, she became angry and resented the baby growing inside her. After the delivery as the baby was placed on her chest, she purposely and forcefully pushed it away. This young lady told me she refused to hold the baby or care for it because she hated the father for what he had done. Can you imagine a tiny little baby caught in a hate relationship? An innocent child was born to a mother who refused to love it or care for it.

Eighteen months later, while conducting a young teen mother program, I was able to help this young mother come to terms with her hate and pain. She cried for a long time, and finally got the courage to tell me this story. I held her and cried with her. Unfortunately, this scenario is not new to me. I have seen it played out far too many times across America in schools throughout the country. I hurt every time I see a young mother trying to raise an unwanted child. I hate to see young children neglected, abused, abandoned, underfed, mistreated and rejected because a young mother did not take into account the "whole" role of what it means to be a parent. So many young people tell me they thought parenting was easier. It's not! Especially when teens are the baby's parents.

Parenting is late-night pacing the floor with a crying baby. It's wondering to yourself. It's changing dirty diapers 10-15 times a day. It's cleaning vomit and diarrhea and seeing it ruin your clothes. It's regular doctor visits and constant attention that a young baby requires. The days of endless time for music, dances, and hanging out with your pals at the mall are limited. I am saddened to see many young mothers with their unwanted babies hanging out at the mall all day, oftentimes without food or water. The young mother seems more worried about her make-up or which guy will notice her than insuring the safety of her baby. Does she respect motherhood? How could she? Parenting? Evidently not!

Don't get me wrong. A baby is a blessing—but parenting takes time, love, patience, and responsibility. I will never forget the baby that died from dehydration (lack of water) while her teen mom was getting her nails done. The baby had just been released from the hospital and the doctor had specifically told the young mother to take the child home, and to continue to feed it fluids to prevent dehydration. Her priorities were cosmetic, not parenting. I wonder what she thinks now whenever she passes by a nail salon. Has she gained her self-respect back or is her child neglect still haunting her?

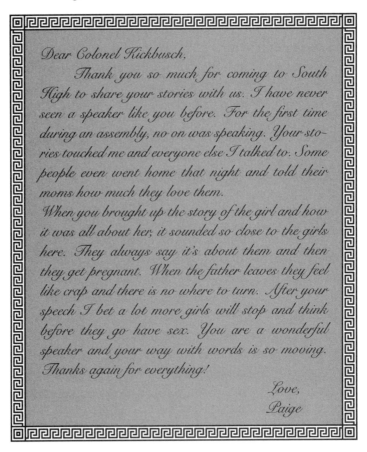

Dear Colonel Kickbusch,

Thank you so much for coming to South High to share your stories with us. I have never seen a speaker like you before. For the first time during an assembly, no on was speaking. Your stories touched me and everyone else I talked to. Some people even went home that night and told their moms how much they love them.

When you brought up the story of the girl and how it was all about her, it sounded so close to the girls here. They always say it's about them and then they get pregnant. When the father leaves they feel like crap and there is no where to turn. After your speech I bet a lot more girls will stop and think before they go have sex. You are a wonderful speaker and your way with words is so moving. Thanks again for everything!

Love,
Paige

And what of the young man who gets involved with the gang—wanting a "family" and thinking this new "family" will support him whenever, whatever, and wherever he

might need them? The following scenario is not uncommon:

A young man is called upon to "prove" himself by shooting a rival gang member. He does as he is told, except that instead of shooting the targeted gang rival he shoots an innocent 7-year-old as she plays in her front yard. And she dies. Who gets the lawyer for him? Who pays the bond money to get him out of jail? Maybe it's his single mother working two jobs to provide shelter, food and clothes for him and his siblings. Maybe the grandparents, aunts, uncles, and godparents all get together and take up a collection of their hard-earned money to bail him out of jail. He stands trial as an adult.

Who goes to court with him? Who speaks on his behalf? Is his "gang family" there for him? Not likely! Now he joins another "family" in prison. He is placed in a cell with someone who will more than likely not treat him like "family." And who will come to visit him in prison, or send him necessities? Will his "gang family" support him? Not likely! It will be his mother, his father, his grandparents, his siblings, his aunts and uncles—his real family—who respect the "real family" relationship.

I taught inside a maximum-security prison for two years in Kansas. My eyes were opened to real truth behind bars. Prisons have a culture unto themselves. I gained the trust of my students. They taught me what it's like to be "caged in" with vicious people. They talked openly about how easily and quickly they can "rape" a young inmate, especially an inexperienced young male. The younger you are, they say, the more attractive a target you become. There is no respect for human dignity in prison.

You may wonder why you haven't heard about these terrible instances. What young male who finally got out

wants to admit to his "homies" that he was raped repeatedly while in prison. Remember he was in a gang because he was tough. Gang members commit a crime because they think they are smart and cunning. Where were his toughness, smartness and cunningness while four grown men pinned him down and stripped him of his manhood. More and more reports are coming out that sexual attacks are occurring in juvenile detention centers where kids as young as 10 are placed!

I want to thank the gentleman who not only shared the raw reality of his violent life behind bars, but also agreed to star in a film I produced entitled *Prison and Education*. It is now used in 27 states in the country as a crime prevention video in schools. There is also the sad reality that many children today have relatives who are also doing time behind bars. This can be devastating to know you have a parent one day and the next day they are gone and will be gone for a long time. When that happens, you are removed from your home and are forced to make many adjustments that bring sadness, guilt, depression and disrespect to your life.

Freedom is one thing you will absolutely miss behind bars. Imagine being stripped of many personal choices such as wearing what you want, eating what you want when you want it, sleeping late, hanging out with your favorite people, and feeling good and safe in the comfort of your home.

Inmates are watched 24 hours a day and the rules never change. They are strict, limiting and harshly enforced. Inmates are forced to live like that for 10 -20 years because they couldn't follow simple and easy rules at home. They refused to respect the rights of others, and now they find themselves in an environment of disrespect, distrust and disgrace.

I know too many young men and women who cry every night in a cold cell trying desperately to hold on to memories of pizza parties, sleep overs, make-up sessions, football games and laughter. Prisons affect the whole family. I can still see the 12-year-old I visited in jail awaiting trial for a drive-by shooting. His question that brought tears to my eyes was "Will I see my mother for Christmas?" Here's a kid who is still a kid but got caught up in the "tough guy" philosophy.

I met a 14-year-old who was giving his mother (a single mom) a terrible time. He went so far as to say things to her that were entirely disrespectful, like "I don't need you, you B---h! I am a man and can take care of myself." His mother approached me, hoping I would say something that would help their relationship. She was at her wit's end. She suspected he was involved in gangs and drugs. Her son wanted to set me straight right way and sarcastically introduced himself by saying, "Look lady I don't need you, and I don't need my mother either. I am a man now, and you think I am just this little punk. Well let me tell you -- you are nobody to me and as far as my mother goes she can go to hell too."

I calmly questioned his so-called independence by asking him who bought the shirt he was wearing? He replied shyly, "My mom." I asked him who bought the nice high top tennis shoes he was wearing? They seemed expensive. Again he replied shyly, "My mom." I kept the tempo up by asking who bought the nice jeans he was wearing? They had no holes and looked like someone had ironed them nicely. He shifted from his arrogant stance and tried to jokingly catch me off guard by saying his aunt had bought them for him

for Christmas. The bottom line was that everything he was wearing was bought by someone else.

Through her tear-filled eyes, his mom apologized for her son's behavior and excused it by saying that her son was resentful toward her because she was raising him alone. His father had abandoned them before he was born, and she had to hold down two minimum wage jobs because she had dropped out of school. She knew first hand how difficult it was to make a living without a college degree. She was determined to get him help because she was trying to avoid another generation of dropouts in her family. By the time I left them, he was showing more respect for his mother—even if it was only to appease me. After we had said our farewells, he glanced back at me. His respectful look told me I had done some good.

I know that during the teen years you experience many different levels of conflict with your parents or guardians. They seem in your eyes to be crazy, out of touch, or say things just to upset you because you think they have nothing better to do than constantly interfere with your life. I am ashamed today to say that once upon a time, I felt this way about my own parents.

I remember one day in particular. My mother, who was raising a large family without the modern luxuries such as dishwasher, microwave, washer/dryer, asked me to help out one day. All she wanted was for me to wash the dishes. I felt incredible rage come over me, and as soon as she was out of my sight I made a horrible gesture towards her. She must

have had eyes in the back of her head, because she asked what I had said. I lied and said something like young people today would say: "Chill out Mom," I said. "I love you, okay? Lie low and be cool, okay?" My mother kept on doing the hard work and no one ever asked her how she felt. No one ever noticed how swollen and sore her feet were from working all day. She did almost all of the housework by herself, because we kids were too selfish, and too disrespectful, to think of anyone else but our so-called busy lives with our friends.

Today, I am an orphan. I have no father or mother. I am all alone now fending for myself. I long so badly for my parents. The best I can do is lay a wreath of flowers at their grave and cry like a baby wishing they were here with me. They loved me—and my nine other brothers and sisters. They fought the drug culture, our peer pressure, the media, the music industry, sex and violence on TV, magazines that exploit the beauty myth which leads young people to become anorexic and bulimic, to name a few of their challenges. They competed with those powerful forces to keep us healthy and alive. Every day they said a prayer of thanks for our safety and well being. When I look back on it, both of my parents had PhD's in parenting. I'm not kidding. They did the best they could with what they had.

The following story is about a young lady who learned what respecting her mom meant after it was too late.

I received an e-mail from a young lady in Ohio. She had listened to my story about respect in a school assembly and she dismissed it as a corny and unrealistic. She wrote about how she had gotten into a bad argument with her mother before going to school because her mother had asked her not to come home late from school. Although her mother was

worried something might happen to her, she yelled at her mother to leave her F%%% alone and back off. She called her mother a vulgar name and pushed her against the refrigerator. When she got on the bus, she bragged to her friends how she had showed her mother who was in charge. She reported how her friends laughed with her and chorused something like: "Yeah, parents suck!"

She went on to say that two weeks later her mom was killed in a car accident. She was now alone and living in a foster home. She went into detail about the day she was removed from her home. She was told that no one in her family wanted her because of her attitude and foul mouth. She had little choice but to live in a strange house. She recalled being given a box to put her possessions in and was told to hurry because she was being relocated as soon as possible. She ran upstairs and the first thing she grabbed was a picture of her mother. She knew the woman who stayed up late at night worrying about her could no longer wait for her. She knew the loving mother who scrapped for extra money to give to her so that she could go to the mall would no longer be able to give her anything.

She remembered walking downstairs, touching the refrigerator and crying. She wished she had said "I'm sorry, Mom—and I love you." She ended her email by saying "Please tell my story to other kids who think they are better off without parents." She added in her P.S.: "I miss my mom." I felt incredible sadness for this young lady. She is a courageous person in my eyes for admitting her mistake and for allowing me to share her tragic story with the hope that you, young reader, will think about how you treat your family.

On the other hand, in an effort to share a balanced perspective to what young people are experiencing at home—yes, there are kids today living with some pretty sick parents. You can't stop alcoholism, drug addiction, domestic violence, sexual abuse, or physical or mental abuse alone. These challenges are beyond your control. In these situations, I believe you are better off living in a safe environment than in a home that is abusive, demeaning and torturous. Please get help for yourself and your family. I hope we can bring respect back into our lives as a core value that has care value.

Reflection Exercises

In this chapter, respect was defined as setting a value on or rating something highly. The following exercises are designed to help you think about the role of respect in your life. Please use the spaces provided to reflect on your own personal experiences, and to determine how respect can guide your decisions and define your values.

1. List examples of how you respect yourself, your family, your community and your country:

   I respect **myself** by: *taking care of my health.*

   I respect **myself** by: *doing the things I say I am going to do.*

   I respect **myself** by: *doing the best that I can do in school.*

   I respect **myself** by:

   I respect **myself** by:

   I respect **myself** by:

   I respect **myself** by:

   I respect **myself** by:

Respect

I respect my **family** by: *always telling them the truth.*

I respect my **family** by: *helping with chores around the house.*

I respect my **family** by: *obeying the rules made by my elders.*

I respect my **family** by:

I respect my **family** by:

I respect my **family** by:

I respect my **family** by:

I respect my **family** by:

I respect my **community** by: *setting a good example for other people my age.*

I respect my **community** by: *participating in projects to help others.*

I respect my **community** by: *picking up trash and cleaning common areas.*

I respect my **community** by:

I respect my **community** by:

I respect my **community** by:

I respect my **community** by:

I respect my **community** by:

I respect my **country** by: *learning about national holidays and heroes.*

I respect my **country** by: *honoring those who serve in the military services.*

I respect my **country** by: *attending school to get a good education.*

I respect my **country** by:

I respect my **country** by:

I respect my **country** by:

I respect my **country** by:

I respect my **country** by:

2. What are your goals for increasing your understanding of respect and the role it plays in your life?

    I will: *go to the library and read about respect.*

I will: *ask a teacher what he/she thinks about respect and discuss it with him/her.*

I will: *ask my parents or relatives or another adult about respect.*

I will :

I will :

I will :

I will :

3. How can you encourage those around you to respect one another more?

I will: *set a good example.*

I will: *respect my self and those around me.*

I will: *observe someone I respect highly and ask for guidance.*

I will :

I will :

I will :

4. It is important to learn from others whom we respect. Who are those people in your life? Name some of them and the reasons for which you respect them below:

PERSON I RESPECT	BECAUSE
Mr. B.	He is a good leader.
Mrs. C.	She is a good adult figure in my life..
Miss D..	She treats me with respect.
Clergyman E..	He keeps the community safe.

5. Write a brief paragraph about why it is important to respect yourself, your family, your community and your country.

El respeto no se compra—se tiene que merecer.

Respect is not bought, it must be earned.

No one can ruin your life. You are always responsible for the way you accept the things that happen to you. The incident is external, the reaction is always your own.

(Eric Butterworth)

Nothing strengthens the judgment and quickens the conscience like individual responsibility.

(Elizabeth Cady Stanton)

If you are given a job you are responsible for doing it. If you say you are going to do something, you had best do it or have a very good reason for not being able to do it. We all had our responsibilities around the house. We could not stand around until we were told to do something. To this day, I can't be idle. I'm constantly doing something.

(Katherine Ortega)

Chapter 8

Responsibility

The amount of freedom you can enjoy depends on your "response-ability" to responsibility.

Many years ago, Montezuma was the ruler of an ancient Aztec civilization in what is now Mexico City. They had mastered astronomy, agriculture, irrigation, the calendar and had constructed towering monuments and pyramids in the jungle which are still standing today. Aztec wise men believed that it was their duty to place a mirror before the people so they might fulfill their responsibilities as citizens, parents and warriors.

Children were raised in a strict manner and were taught specific lessons in the form of stories, anecdotes and rhymes. The following story is in keeping with that ancient tradition. It is adapted from a story told by Yolanda Nava in her book, *It's All in the Frijoles*. In it, 100 famous Latinos share their real life stories, time-tested dichos, favorite folk-

tales and inspiring words of wisdom. The story I have selected is one you will want to remember.

Many, many years ago there was a small boy who never listened to his parents. Although his parents tried their best to teach him to honor his Mexican American heritage and to accept his family responsibilities, he refused to listen. Pleas by his grandparents and friends fell on deaf ears. Emiliano had made up his mind that he didn't have to listen to anyone.

One morning, Emiliano ran away from home. He hoped to find someone who wouldn't tell him what to do. He ran far away from his barrio, past all of the houses, and down the path deep into a nearby woods. He wandered deeper and deeper until he came upon a small house in a clearing. On the front porch sat a short, round old man in a rocking chair.

The youngster walked up to the porch and noticed that the old man was watching his every move. The runaway took a step closer and saw that the old man was patiently waiting for his visitor to speak.

"I'd like something to eat," said Emiliano.

The old man stared at the young boy a moment before he spoke, then commented, "Oh, you would, would you?"

"That's right," responded Emiliano, "I'm hungry. I'd like something to eat."

The old man had heard stories about the youngster from people he knew in the barrio. If this is the same boy, the old man thought to himself, I must hold up a mirror so he can see how he should behave around others. The old man leaned forward in his chair.

"I have heard much about you, young man. You need to stop being so irresponsible. No one will like being around you unless you change your ways."

The youngster only laughed.

At that, the old man smiled his understanding. "You look hungry, so I will feed you. Come in. I've got some sandwich meat and chips. All I've got to drink is water, though. But you are welcome to it. And if you want, you can spend the night."

The youngster followed his host into the house.

The next morning, the old man announced he had some shopping to do in town. "Listen, mijo, while I am, gone the only thing I must ask you to do is to put beans on to cook in the pot. Be careful, though. Do not put more than 13 beans in the pot to boil. Do you understand?"

The boy nodded.

"I'll be back in an hour or so," the old man assured him. "My friend, Maria, is on her way over here. When she arrives, you can start the bean soup."

When the old man left, the boy decided to start without Maria. He filled the pot with water and put it on the burner. Carefully he counted out 13 beans and tossed them in.

"That doesn't seem like many beans," he said aloud. "That's hardly enough beans for a spoonful, let alone a meal. There won't be enough to eat unless I add more."

He found more beans in the cupboard and threw in several dozen more. When the water started to boil, the beans swelled up, first filling the pot, then overflowing onto the stove and spilling onto the floor. Quickly he grabbed another pot and divided the beans, but the beans swelled so much the second pot overflowed. By the time Maria got there, the kitchen was a mess.

They were unable to clean the kitchen in time to prevent the old man from seeing the mess.

"Why didn't you do as I asked?" he addressed the boy.

"It was her fault," the boy protested, pointing to Maria, whose jaw dropped in astonishment.

"Maria. Did you add more beans to the pot?" the old man asked, knowing full well that Emiliano wasn't telling the truth.

"No, sir," she announced meekly.

"Emiliano?" he asked, turning his attention on the nervous youngster.

"Emiliano what?" the boy answered sarcastically.

"Finish the cleanup you've started. Maria, I need you to run into town for something I forgot."

The old man didn't say anything else about the incident the rest of the evening. The next morning, the old man told Emiliano he had to give a speech at the university and that he would return later that afternoon. He advised the youngster to wait for Maria before he boiled the second set of beans.

"How many beans?" the old man quizzed.

"Thirteen."

"Good! No more, no less. And, by the way, you are welcomed to play in the yard, take the canoe out on the lake or read in my library while I am gone. However, if you go into the library, do not open the large book with the red cover. I'll only be gone a couple of hours."

"Yeah. Yeah. Whatever!" the boy replied.

The old man waited until Maria arrived before he left. The boy was unaware that the old man had called his parents and that he would be bringing them back with him when he returned.

The red book on the card table intrigued Emiliano. He waited until Maria looked in the closet for the shoes he said he had put in there, and then locked her inside. He rushed into the library and sat in a chair next to the book.

"It's locked!" he said angrily. "The old man locked it."

After working with it for awhile, he managed to pry it open. He could make out the words "Power" and "masterful," but the rest of the language was hard to decipher.

"No wonder the old man didn't want me to open this book," the youngster rationalized. "It looks like something very important."

He leafed through the book until he got to a book-marked page.

"I wonder what this says."

"Emiliano," came a voice from the closet. "If you've got the master's red book, you'd better put it down."

Emiliano smiled.

"So it is important. What would happen if I read this highlighted passage?"

"Emiliano. Put the book up," cautioned Maria from the locked closet.

No sooner had the boy read the highlighted passage than strange things began to happen. Suddenly he was surrounded by ghastly ghostly figures which frightened him into a catatonic stupor.

When the old man returned with the boy's parents, they found him frozen to the chair with the red book on his lap.

Responsibility

"He did the very thing I told him not to do," lamented the old man. Maria's shouts from her temporary confinement aroused their attention and she was freed. The old man explained to the boy's parents that Emiliano must have misread one of the incantations from the holy book and placed a spell upon himself.

"I will try my best to free your son, but I can make no promises. He may have to pay a severe penalty for his irresponsible trespass in an area that requires a considerable amount of training and education."

The old man was able to remedy the situation and save the boy from an institutionalized existence.

"You are very fortunate, my son," said the boy's father. "This man has saved you from a life of misery."

"Father. Mother," the boy shouted. "I 'm so happy to see you. I did something I shouldn't have. I was so frightened."

He turned to the old man.

"I'm sorry. I'll never do that again. Thank you for saving my life."

The old man patted the youngster on the head and smiled. "Your apology only works if you promise me you will no longer disobey your parents. You must become a responsible young adult. Grownups ask you to do certain things because they know what is best for you."

"I promise to listen and take responsibility for my words and actions," assured Emiliano.

"I believe you," replied the old man as he winked at the boy's parents.

The healthy youngster returned home with his parents. From that day on, Emiliano made himself useful to his parents, his brothers and sisters, his teachers and his barrio.

He became very well-known and respected. He epitomized responsibility and taught younger kids how to be more responsible. He remembered fondly the lessons he had learned from the old man who could make and break spells, and talk with the spirits.

This old story captures the essence of both responsibility and irresponsibility: there cannot be freedom without responsibility. The more responsible we are, the more personal autonomy and freedom we will enjoy. It's as simple – or as hard – as that. Another way of looking at it is what is your "response-ability" to the amount of freedom you are given? How often have you limited your own freedom by acting irresponsibly? For example, how many times have we heard the words, "I didn't mean to hit her" or "the gun just went off; I didn't mean to shoot it." Or "I didn't see that red light" or "I didn't understand the assignment, so I just didn't do it." Common phrases, yet they describe actions that can bring bad consequences.

We all have responsibilities at home also. What are they? Maybe it is to maintain our living areas on a daily basis – no clothes on the floor, the shoes in the closet, the books, not strewn around the room. In addition, we may have assigned tasks, such as washing the dishes after dinner, taking the trash out, helping out with the lawn. A major responsibility is to respect our parents and what they provide for us.

I once spoke at a high school where there was such anger within and outside certain groups, that the event ended up in a disturbance that required police officers to be called upon to restore the peace. It was unfortunate -- this did not have to happen. If these young people had respected where they were, respected their teachers and parents, respected their environment, and behaved in a responsible manner; it would have been a beautiful event. As it turned out, teachers, parents, and other students were embarrassed and the disrespectful young people were taken away in police cars. No one gained anything from the spectacle.

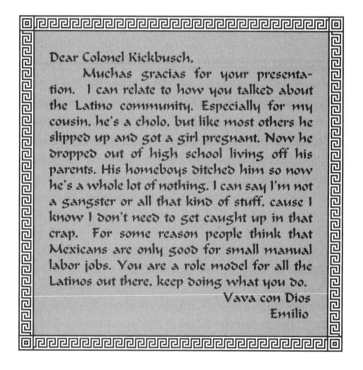

Dear Colonel Kickbusch,

Muchas gracias for your presentation. I can relate to how you talked about the Latino community. Especially for my cousin, he's a cholo, but like most others he slipped up and got a girl pregnant. Now he dropped out of high school living off his parents. His homeboys ditched him so now he's a whole lot of nothing. I can say I'm not a gangster or all that kind of stuff, cause I know I don't need to get caught up in that crap. For some reason people think that Mexicans are only good for small manual labor jobs. You are a role model for all the Latinos out there, keep doing what you do.

Vava con Dios
Emilio

We not only have responsibility for ourselves, but we have responsibility for others as well. Community service is a wonderful way to get involved and to contribute to our community. There are hospitals and nursing homes needing

assistance with activities for their patients. There are literacy programs in almost every area of the country needing assistance from those who can teach English skills to non-English speaking people who are willing to learn. Some schools offer mentoring programs that can be a great way to be involved in helping someone else through some rough times.

In his thoroughly inspiring book, *Rock, Paper, Scissors,* Sheldon Kopp explores the personal dilemma of accepting responsibility for whatever happens to us regardless of the circumstances: He says:

> *My wish is only that (people) understand that personal power doesn't come from trying to control external events and other people. A person cannot do what cannot be done. Life is not a matter to be managed. We have (limited) influence on its outcomes. Our only impact lies in how we live it. We didn't ask for the responsibility of taking charge of ourselves, but it's an important responsibility nonetheless. And, in the end, no matter how well we have prepared, the moment belongs to the quality of our choices.*

In the story I used to introduce this chapter, that's what happened to Emiliano. He became free when he became more responsible. He realized that the consequences of his disrespectful behavior could have gotten him institutionalized. It was his good fortune that the old master could break spells. In real life, the consequences of irresponsible behavior can ruin our lives. Sometimes "spells can't be broken."

Don't become another tragic story like the young man who wanted to pierce his ear because piercing was in. He used the same needle his buddies used. While drinking beer he got the courage and support from his so-called buddies.

Little did he know that one of his buddies was HIV-positive. He is now HIV-positive and faces a tough life ahead.

I encourage you to take full responsibility for your thoughts, beliefs and actions. Ask yourself if you are seeing life through "peer lenses" or through your own eyes. Be your own person. Take responsibility for your own growth and development by recognizing that freedom, autonomy, independence and responsibility go hand in hand. They always have and they always will.

Reflection Exercises

1. How many times have you heard the following statements?

   She makes me mad.

   He hurt my feelings.

   You make me happy.

   I couldn't study because of him.

   I didn't have a choice.

   Think of a situation you have experienced recently in which you found yourself expressing these same, or similar, sentiments. If you expressed these viewpoints, you were not taking responsibility for your actions. Why? Because no one can make you irresponsible without your permission. Rephrase each of these statements and relate your answer to the personal situation you thought of earlier. Complete each of these sentences:

   I chose to get angry because:

   I felt sad, depressed, betrayed (you fill in the
      blank) because:

   I am happy because:

   I chose not to study because:

   I chose to handle the situation this way
      because:

2. Complete the following statements:

I tend to avoid responsibility when:

I can usually avoid an unpleasant
   responsibility by:

The way I feel about certain responsibilities is:

I have some ideas and feelings I'd like to
   share with others, but:

I would be happy to assume more responsibility
   if my parents/teachers would:

I can act very responsibly when:

Right now, the way I feel about responsibility is:

*When you become responsible, you
increase your "response-ability."*

No matter what your work, let it be your own. Let it be in your bones. In that way you will open the door by which the affluence of heaven and earth shall stream into you.

[Ralph Waldo Emerson]

In order to burn out, a person needs to have been on fire at one time.

[Ayala Pines]

If you want something, you have to work for it. It's not going to be given to you without any effort... Never be afraid of hard work. It's good for the soul.

[Loretta Sanchez]

Chapter 9

Work Ethic

"Always do a job so well that even when you are not there your work will speak for you.
(My Mother)

Simply stated, a healthy work ethic is ethics applied to work environments. This work may include going to school or college. People who have a strong work ethic know that it isn't the luck of the draw that determines their success in life. They know there isn't much guesswork involved in getting the results they want. Whether those results are good grades, more freedom and independence, a good job, respect, a loving family, promotion potential, and so on.

A school example of work ethic may be a student (we'll call him Garth) who has a report that is due the following day, yet he has worked on it sporadically. As a result Garth has only two pages of a ten-page report completed. The assignment was given a month ago, either in class or was

listed on the class syllabus. During the intervening time, Garth has hung out with his friends, gone to the movies a few times, played pool at the regular hangout, slept late and had "fun." Now he realizes the report is due and, obviously, whatever he turns in will not be first quality. Garth lacks an important ingredient for success in school and in life—he lacks a healthy work ethic.

Garth is not the only one with a poor work ethic. Mary, an employee of ABC Company calls in sick on Mondays after a long weekend at the coast. Other employees must "cover" for her to be sure the work gets done. Mary does this often enough that it aggravates her fellow employees, but she is within the company policy of not calling in sick more than three Mondays within a working quarter of the year. She barely complies with the policy. She is not practicing a good work ethic. Even worse, she knows she is abusing the rules, and yet is willing to inconvenience her fellow employees.

A good rule of measure for a first job is to show up early, well groomed (nice haircut, polished shoes or clean tennis shoes, ironed shirt and skirt or dress). First impressions are extremely important; so it is best to be a conservative dresser (leave the nose rings and earrings at home). By arriving early, you show your willingness and this shows that you are:

❖ Responsible
❖ Disciplined
❖ Not afraid of hard work
❖ Willing to give 110%

All of these are characteristics of people who want to be successful in life. The following true story is about a young man who said he was willing to work hard and do

anything to prove he was a good worker. So he was asked to sweep the floor. The young man came early to work and worked long hours, even closing the store. He learned all about being a McDonald's employee. The boss asked him, "What do you want out of life?" The young man replied that he wanted to work hard to make something of himself. Today, that young man owns a McDonald's restaurant.

There are many opportunities to learn a strong work ethic. For example: My mother worked as a hotel maid, and one of her tasks was cleaning toilets. She scrubbed them until they sparkled. Someone asked her, "Why do you work so hard to polish and clean that toilet? No one will notice it and no one will appreciate your hard work."

She answered: "You never know who will see your work, so do it well and there will never be a doubt as to who did it."

What my mother meant was that our work speaks for us. What we put into the task at hand, whether it is a project at work or at school, will tell others about the kind of person we are—our attitude, our caring, our ability and willingness to work hard. No job is too trivial. If you look at a school project as "not worth doing it right," you will earn the reward (a grade) equal to the work you put into it. Sooner or later we pay for talking the easy way out. Having a good work ethic will always reward us. Sometimes it takes time for those rewards to come to us, but please take it from someone who has worked all of her life—having a good work ethic works!

Keep working toward your dream even if you are the only one who believes in your dream.

Famous health educator and enthusiast, Jack LaLanne,
studied pre-med in college and planned to become a medical

doctor. However, he realized that the medical profession was focused on recovery after illness instead of prevention before illness. He was interested in helping people prevent illness by maintaining a healthy lifestyle centered on personal fitness. That was his dream.

At age twenty-one he opened the nation's first health studio in an old brick office building in Oakland, California. The sports equipment he invented is standard issue in health spas today. He was the first to encourage women, people with physical disabilities and the elderly to exercise for health.

His methods were criticized by the medical profession, the sports community and the media—until it was obvious that LaLanne was on to something. His strong work ethic sustained him for fifty years. When he was asked recently what made his fitness program so successful, he said, "I understand the working of the body, the muscles and bones, the nerves...What I was doing then, and continue to do now, is scientifically correct...starting with a healthy diet—and today everyone knows it. It was my dream of a healthy America that carried me through."

A young girl who grew up in rural Mississippi dreamed of becoming a TV news personality. Although she had an extremely unhappy childhood, including abuse, she held on to her media dream. She became a rebellious and uncontrollable teenager. As a last resort, her mother sent her to live with her father, Vernon Winfrey. Both he and his wife,

Zelma, were disciplinarians. They taught Oprah the importance of education, discipline and fairness.

Oprah finished high school and entered Tennessee State
University. She majored in speech communications and
landed a job at WTVF-TV in Baltimore, Maryland and
co-anchored the Six O'clock News.

Several years later, Oprah hosted the talk show AM
Chicago, which was renamed The Oprah Winfrey Show.
Eventually, she purchased her own talk show from Capital
Cities/ABC and it quickly became the number-one talk show
in America. She describes her success this way: "I had a
vision I could succeed at anything I decided to do. You have
to believe you can be whatever your heart desires and be
willing to work for it."

In his book, *Wisdom of the Ages*, Wayne Dyer explains
the relationship between our work, life and purpose. He
says:

*When you are born into this world your work is born
with you. You have been made for some particular
work, and the desire for that work was put into your
heart at the moment you showed up here. If you are
unable to feel connected to that purpose because you
have opted to do something that you don't love,
regardless of how all that got started or what keeps
you there today, you can benefit greatly by listening to
what…your soul prompts you to do.*

Dear Colonel Kickbusch,

I liked your speech because you were talking about real life situations that happen in people's life, and you know what is going through our (young people) minds. The story I liked the most was the one about the girl that didn't appreciate her mom... My mom only wants to make me happy and I don't appreciate it for what it's worth. Your speech opened my eyes to show her how much I love her and it also showed me that we should tell them that we love them every second because we are not guaranteed tomorrows and not to take life for granted. Thank you for inspiring me so much with those stories, you have also inspired me to go far in life just like you did and not let anyone hold me back from what I want to achieve.

Thank you,
Alma

Having a good work ethic means you understand and value how important it is to do a good job. And, as Wayne Dyer tells us, it can lead to your special life work. What if you have never worked in your life? I see many students today who have it pretty easy because their parents can afford just about everything kids ask for. I find it interesting that teens now expect to own and drive a car at sixteen. Who pays for this luxury? What about the expensive insurance? Who worries about paying the bill? I learned from the consumer bureau that the average teenager spends fifty dollars

a week! Again, where does this money come from? What will happen when you are on your own and suddenly, you are faced with harsh realities like paying rent, food, clothes, cable TV, high speed Internet, phone, water, light, gas, car insurance, mental and dental medical plans, taxes, credit cards and so on?

Unless you are what society today calls an inheritance baby (by the way, they are spending their inheritance at the rate of $10,000 a day), you will be much better off learning while you are young how important it is to have a strong work ethic. I provide training and consulting for companies in America. The number-one challenge of young employees today is facing the fact that they have to work hard to get ahead, and that it takes time to make the big bucks.

This reality frustrates many young employees because they are used to having it all too soon and too young. My own daughter enlightened me one evening by saying that "parents have created a world of deception by leading young people to believe that things come easy. Then suddenly, we have to look at life as not being that easy." These words came from a young lady with whom I insisted on getting a job at sixteen.

Apparently, we make it too easy for young people and then expect them to "get with the program" of working hard and doing things right. I encourage you, young reader, to give yourself the greatest gift of all: Get a job and see how hard it is to make a dollar. I guarantee that you will respect money, and that you will gain an incredible work ethic that will serve you well in the future. I learned an interesting thing from a *Fortune* magazine article: of the top ten moneymakers in the world, five came from humble backgrounds that required them to work as young people.

I started working when I was twelve and remember the great job it gave me to give my entire earnings to my father

who was struggling financially to support us. While you may not be faced with this situation, working can still help provide you with great pride in yourself. Don't expect all of the money to come from your parents. Do your share at home. Remember you are living rent-free, food-free, utilities-free, your clothes are bought by your parents, etc. Can you pay your parents back for what they provide for you on a daily basis? It's easier than you think. Showing a good work ethic with your schoolwork, at home, and in your part time job is a great way of saying thanks to your parents.

I have come to realize that the essence of work—the right work—is to understand that its importance lies not only in what we have done or are doing, but who we have become because we honored our work ethic. Finding fulfillment in our work, no matter what kind of work it is, is a spiritual experience. That was my father's philosophy and it is mine, too. To have a strong work ethic—to feel that what we are doing is right for ourselves, for our growth and development and good for the world at the same time can be one of the great triumphs of our lives.

I'm going to share something most books on work ethics don't mention, and especially books written with a young adult audience in mind. I believe work is a spiritual activity—we are constantly asking ourselves if we are in the right line of work. I am quite serious in my belief that work is spiritual. The phrase *laborae est orare* (to labor is to pray), written by St. Benedict some 1,400 years ago, is still a powerful insight. I believe young people are much more spiritual than older people give them credit for and wonder if you, young reader, have ever considered the spiritual nature of work. If St. Benedict is right, and I believe he is, our work is a kind of prayer. And as prayer, it is charged with meaning and value.

144

My father was a minister for 40 years and I can attest to his strong work ethic. My father worked with his hands for 83 years without complaint. I was taught to work hard and to have a healthy respect for work. I am fortunate indeed to love what I do for a living and I will do my best to help you gain that same sense of satisfaction.

One of the keys to any possible happiness and success in work is to have a strong work ethic and to nurture it no matter what type of work you are doing, because it will lead you to the work you are meant to do. Many of the jobs you will take as a young person are not what you are called to do because they are usually after school jobs. But you must do them well if you expect to find your true calling. I can tell you from personal experience that work can be difficult and dramatic. It is a high-stakes game in which our identity, self-esteem, self-worth and ability to make a decent living unfold.

Work — any work, all work — is where we can make ourselves or break ourselves. But I will share a secret with you: It is a making and unmaking that cannot be measured by money, status, power and position alone. We can earn fortunes or lose them, build our reputations or lose them, ensure our health or ruin it. We can choose to work or run away from it. But work is a pilgrimage. It is a journey to express or hide our talents and abilities. We can test our skills or hide our worth.

Good work, done well for the right reasons, has always been and always will be a sign of inner and outer maturity. It is our gift to our family, our community, our society and ourselves. Without a strong work ethic, you will fail — and you will disappoint those who love and depend upon you. By honoring your work ethic, you honor your parents, your family and your higher self.

Reflection Exercises

1. Set aside fifteen minutes. Take a blank sheet of paper and write at the top of it: *The most important things I have learned about work are…*

    Write as many of your ideas as you can in the next ten minutes. During the last five minutes, decide what the five most important things are and write them in the space below:

2. Take another look at the top five choices you listed above. In the space provided below, describe how each of those insights helped you to be more successful on the job and in school.

3. Complete the following statements:
   I am willing to work because:

   I got my work ethic from:
      who taught me:

   Earlier in this chapter, you said work can
   make you or break you. Well, work has:
   me because:

   The people I admire the most for their strong
   work ethic are:
      because:

   I have held some kind of job since I was :

      and believe everyone should:

   What I like most about my current job is:

      and I believe everyone should:

   The most important thing I learned from this
      chapter is:

*You must maintain a strong
work ethic in the midst of your
business and busyness.*

We must remain disciplined and we must succeed or our children and grandchildren will one day rightfully ask why we did not give our best efforts. [Arthur Ashe]

If you have the discipline, you will be liberated by it. [Peter Hall]

Mighty mountain ranges and landscapes are sculpted by the power of tiny, disciplined droplets of rain. [Edward deBono]

Chapter 10

Self-Discipline

*Self-disciplined people turn
"idle" moments into "ideal"
moments.*

Have you ever set goals, made New Year's resolutions, or promised someone—or yourself—that you were going to do something to improve your life? If you're like most young people your intentions are good, but your follow-through usually ends up lacking the drive and determination to keep your promises or achieve your stated goals.

It's easy to excitedly announce your plans to launch a bold, new self-development venture complete with checklists, good intentions and due dates. But the real test of your commitment comes 30, 60, or 120 days later. Most young people rarely have the self-discipline to turn their intentions

into something more than *wishcraft*. It's okay to wish for something, but you've got to turn those wishes into actions. Otherwise, the spark that ignited your intense desire will fizzle to an ember once the initial glow wears off.

Studies of energetic, thriving young people show that they are self-disciplined and persistent when it comes to working toward their goals. Less successful young adults, however, seem to lose interest and allow themselves to be distracted. The Nobel Prize winning French philosopher, physician and musician, Albert Schweitzer fervently believed "the tragedy of life is what dies inside people while they live." For many young people, their passion and spirit seems to slip away when the excitement wears off.

Although we all have our "doubt days" or visit "Pity City" when we're feeling tired and vulnerable, young adults who are determined and self-disciplined bounce back quickly and move undeterred toward keeping their promises and meeting their goals in life. In the following story a young man learned the importance of disciplined, hard work and of the benefits it gave him.

He lived in a small hut on a knoll about a mile from a huge walnut grove. His father was a laborer and one of his father's jobs was to shake the nuts from the trees by using a long hook. Anthony's job was to separate the nuts from their peels and bag them. His hands were browned by the sun and the walnut juice and blistered by the hard work. But five-year-old Anthony loved to work beside his father.

Like most immigrant families, his family moved from plantation to plantation. They picked everything: nuts, tomatoes, lettuce, lemons, oranges, grapes and cotton. He stood behind huge thrashing machines and picked beans with one hand while shielding his face from the dirt and

debris with the other. His father taught him about responsibility, honest work and self-discipline. I will let Anthony talk about his childhood field hand experiences:

> *Like gypsies we vagabonded from one home to the next. We carried our home on our backs. I will never lose the feeling of waking before the sun, and tromping down to the fields with my father, of wanting to please him and my mother, and helping them provide for our family. It was a magical thing. It did not matter where we were or what we picked. What mattered was that we had a job to do—together—and that my family needed me. By our combined, disciplined efforts we made a life out of no life at all.*

Anthony was born in Chihuahua, Mexico in 1915. He began his acting career at the age of twenty as a means of improving his English. I'm sure you've heard of this actor, writer and producer. In his candid biography, One Man Tango, Anthony Quinn captures the importance of how honest, disciplined work contributes to our autonomy and independence. Like me, he never lost sight of his roots; and like me, he is the product of a hard-working family that understood the value of self-discipline over the long haul.

If you want to be more self-disciplined in order to get rid of some self-destructive habits like smoking, weekend drinking, casual sex, drugs, or loafing, you've got to manage your way out of them. Self-discipline is more than a

thought process. It is an act of will. You've got to have more will power than won't power. You've got to do more than just say no!

You will have to face great temptations, peer pressure and your own self-doubt and undisciplined nature. You've got to have a plan to be somewhere else on Friday and Saturday nights instead of at a party where alcohol and drugs are served. You've got to have a specific reason for not getting into the backseat of a car with someone who doesn't understand the negative consequences of casual sex. You've got to care enough about your own health and well being to stop putting cigarettes in your mouth or unhealthy food in your stomach.

Don't continue to do drugs or hang out with people who do. Most young people who do drugs do them to fit in with the crowd. How can you fit in if you don't understand yourself well enough to know who's fitting in? Most people drug themselves up because they feel so down. And the more they get high, the lower they feel. Unfortunately, drug abuse is soul abuse. Every hit you take (and hit is the right word) is the terrible price you pay for sabotaging your happiness and success.

If you are caving in to peer pressure to do drugs, have premarital sex, defy your parents, give your teachers a hard time, (if you are in school at all), drink yourself unconscious or steal something to prove your worth, you have sold out! You have chosen to dishonor yourself and block your potential. That's a loaded sentence so you may want to read it again. Slowly and thoughtfully. Close the door on anything or anyone who chooses to abuse you, hurt you or use you. Close the door. Lock it and throw away the key.

Helen Nearing, in her insightful book, *Loving and Leaving the Good Life,* writes:

Self-Discipline

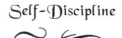

When one door closes, another opens...into another room, another space, other happenings. There are many doors to open and close in our lives. Some we leave ajar, when we hope and plan to return. Some doors are slammed shut decisively...some are closed regretfully, softly...Closing a door means opening onto new vistas and ventures, new possibilities, new incentives.

Helen Nearing is right. Closing doors, slamming them if you have to, on self-destructive habits, interests and relationships will open new opportunities for you in other more life-affirming areas.

All it takes is a little self-discipline and faith in yourself. (You'll read more about faith in Chapter Thirteen—it's the spiritual "glue" that makes self-discipline worthwhile.) Chose the areas in your life in which you want to become more disciplined. For example, choose to be more disciplined in your thinking, feeling and actions.

Disciplined Thinking

Adopt a positive attitude no matter what happens. Most young people don't keep track of the number of thoughts they have each day which are negative in nature. There is a considerable amount of internal dialogue that hums constantly in our brains—over 62,000 thoughts, according to behavioral psychologists.

Unfortunately, most of the mental "chatter" is negative because most of us grow up in negative environments. Our schools, churches, homes and jobs are filled with negative messages like, "Don't do this" and "Don't do that," or "Don't rock the boat." Young people who seem to have it all

together focus on "Do's" instead of "Don'ts." They concentrate on what they can do instead of what they can't. They know that the changes they want to make in their lives are one thought away, and that positive thoughts lead to choices that usually bring positive outcomes.

Whenever a negative thought about your abilities, talents or self-worth enters your mind, say to yourself: "I am a good person who has a very special purpose." It is okay to psych yourself up—to sell yourself on yourself! People who are successful do it all the time. They refuse to stay depressed or worried. When they catch themselves saying or thinking negative things about themselves they ask themselves why they are choosing to allow someone or something to upset them.

Remember—you are the sum total of all of the thoughts, choices and actions you have ever made. If you want to change the way you are, where you are and who you are—change your thinking. Be careful of your thoughts, they may become your future at any moment.

Disciplined Feeling

Controlling our emotions is a sign of maturity. Unfortunately, from a very young age we are taught that some emotions are "bad" and that it is not appropriate to feel or show them. Strong emotions such as fear, anger and jealousy are viewed as negative. Since we are told things like "It's not nice to be mad," or "Stop crying," or "Big boys aren't afraid," etc., we learn to suppress these emotions. We hold these strong feelings inside until one day we erupt with anger and hostility.

The important thing to remember about emotions is that emotions in and of themselves are not wrong. They just

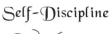

are! Emotions can show us that a particular situation isn't right, that something needs to be said or done, that we are either comfortable or uncomfortable with what is going on or about to happen. Emotions help us express our thoughts so people can understand us. Sometimes our emotions are intense and straight forward, and other times it can be difficult for other people to "read" us.

One thing is for sure—what worries you, or causes you to "lose your cool," or frightens you, or causes you to doubt yourself, or makes you feel guilty, masters you. Uncontrolled emotions are choices based on the negative beliefs we have about our ability to deal with a particular situation and with our own negative self-esteem. You will be able to control your emotions once you know that no one can make you fearful, angry or anxious without your consent.

Disciplined Action

Every action you take, each gesture you make, everything you do, is either a victory or a defeat in your journey to be what you are supposed to be. Actions really do speak louder than words, and people judge you on what they see you do. Are your thoughts, beliefs and actions in sync or do your acts contradict your beliefs and values? Do you confuse activity with accomplishment?

People who are going places have two important traits, a vision and a plan. So where are you going and how are you going to get there? Does your daily satisfaction meter register high in happiness and accomplishments or low in missed opportunities and fulfillment? How disciplined are you when it comes to saying no to drugs and alcohol, pre-marital sex, skipping work or school, blaming someone else for your troubles, or giving your parents a hard time? When

is the last time you refused to eat high fat, high cholesterol foods? On a scale from one-to-ten with ten being very disciplined, how self-disciplined are you?

> Dear Colonel Kickbusch,
>   I would like to thank you for coming to Omaha South High School. I really thought it would be another boring speech. I missed out on taking my math test to come listen to you. I really think it was worth it, since I have grown just that little bit mentally now....
>   Sean

I'm going to tell you something that I hope you have enough faith in me to believe: *Self-discipline is self care.* Being disciplined enough to stand up for your beliefs, keep your promises and be true to yourself is a cornerstone in your journey toward a happy, healthy and successful life. If you've read this far in this book, you've got the discipline it takes to follow through on commitments. It will be your disciplined approach to the things that matter in your life which will help you turn *idle* minutes into *ideal* moments. Remember that Goal Setting needs to be Realistic, Supportive and Measurable.

Reflection Exercises

1. Learn to sell yourself on yourself by speaking highly of yourself. I don't mean being egotistical or narcissistic. I'm talking about a disciplined approach to psyching yourself up when you feel down or suffer a setback. Run through the alphabet and identify positive words that correspond with the letters in the alphabet. Then preface each word with the phrase *I am*. For example: *I am* attractive. *I am* brilliant. I am creative. *I am* disciplined. *I am* enthusiastic. Complete the following positive *I am* statements, beginning with the letter "f:"

   I am f_____   I am m_____
   I am g_____   I am n_____
   I am h_____   I am o_____
   I am i_____   I am p_____
   I am j_____   I am r_____
   I am k_____   I am s_____
   I am l_____   I am t_____

Repeat these positive phrases to yourself as often as you can through the day. Use them as affirmations. If you are disciplined enough to use them every day, you will notice a definite difference in the way you see yourself.

2. Here are some examples of self-discipline statements many of the students I have met in schools throughout America use to remind themselves to keep their commitments and promises. See how many of them you can adopt to help you become a "discipline warrior," too:

I will not drink and drive.

I will not take advantage of or ridicule people less fortunate than myself.

I will treat everyone I meet with dignity and respect.

I will keep my promises and honor my commitments.

I will not steal what is not mine.

I will honor my parents, brothers and sisters.

I will work every day to improve my talents and abilities.

I will:

I will:

I will:

I will:

I will:

I will:

3. Complete the following statements:

By being more self-disciplined, I believe I can:

Once I am able to do that, I believe my life will change in the following ways:

In order for me to be more self-disciplined, I've got to:

By this time next week, I'm going to be more disciplined at:

A month from now, I will have benefited from my disciplined approach in the following ways:

Self-discipline is self-care consistently administered.

Everyone has special interests and areas in which they have creative talents.

[Howard Gardner]

The kernel of creativity is there in the infant: the desire and drive to explore, to find out about things, to try things out, to experiment with different ways of handling things and looking at things. As they grow older, children begin to create entire universes of reality in their play.

[Teresa Amabile]

Your imagination is your preview of life's coming attractions.

[Albert Einstein]

Chapter 11

Creativity

The creative mind leaps, doubles back, circles and dives from one idea to the next.

In their outstanding book, *Encouraging the Heart,* James Kouzes and Barry Posner share the story about Sonya Lopes, a school reform coordinator at the Turnbull Learning Academy, a public elementary school in San Mates, California. She decided that the students and faculty needed to have more fun. She had read Dave Hemsath and Leslie Yerke's book, *301 Ways to Have Fun at Work,* and put some of the author's suggestions to work. As she put it, "I'm an advisor-critic-listener-reflective partner-confidante to the principal. I felt we needed a more proactive approach in the search for fun opportunities—for everyone! So I improvised."

She posted the word *FUN* in very conspicuous location she could find: on her office door, on the principal's door, in the hallways, as a bookmark in her planner, on staff meet-

ing room walls. One week she asked colleagues to return their "regular old staff questionnaires" by folding them into airplanes and flying them to her. She cheerfully announced that "for the first time ever, everyone returned his or her questionnaire.

The PTA got involved and decorated the staff restrooms, hallways and the cafeteria with potpourri, colorful wall hangings and posters. "What I learned," said Lopes, "was that by encouraging the hearts of others, I encourage myself. When I walked around the school smiling at everyone I met and calling them by their names, I became uplifted. I made muffins and attached notes to them as spirit lifters for teachers. Morale soared. Smiles escalated. The school was filled with lightness and fun.

Sonya Lopes used her creativity to transform an elementary school into a fun-filled learning institution. She used a creative approach to add a little spice and excitement to an otherwise dull school day. The students benefited and so did a school administration. The school also found that the parents of the students were just waiting for an opportunity to get more involved in making the school environment a learning environment that endorsed fun as well.

The purpose of this chapter is to help you believe in your own creative ability and adopt creativity as one of your core values, not just during your school years, but for the rest of your life. You will find that most of your achievements in life will come from your creative insights as much, if not more, than your rational thinking.

When I ask students across America to name someone who is creative, most give the following names: Albert Einstein, Thomas Edison, George Washington Carver, Alexander Graham Bell, Walt Disney, Michelangelo and Norman Rockwell. When asked to name people in recent times who are considered as creative, young people usually refer to persons such as Bill Cosby, Jim Hensen, Steven Speilberg, Steve Jobs, David Copperfield and Robin Williams.

Creative labels are usually assigned to well-known inventors, artists, writers, entertainers, musicians, comedians and scientists. Some people seem to be more creative than others, but it's because they use their creativity instead of hiding it. We are all creative. Being creative is part of our nature, but we have to let our creativity shine. Chuck Jones, the animator who created Wile E. Coyote the cartoon character, says that in order to draw a coyote, you have to "have a coyote inside of you…And it's your job to get it out…You have to find the coyote within you."

Has this ever happened to you? You're out for a walk, riding a bike, resting alone or jogging. All of a sudden into your head pops a solution to a problem that's been troubling you for a couple of weeks. You think to yourself, "Why didn't I think of that before?"

In such moments you've made contact with the creative spirit, that illusive genius of good—and sometimes great—ideas. When our creative spirit stirs, it energizes us and fills us with a desire to create something worthwhile. No matter who you are, you can be a product from a *barrio*, one parent family, (no parent family), large family, small family or rich neighborhood—the creative spirit can enter your life—if you let it. It is at hand for anyone who wants to tinker, to explore, to leave things better than they are.

The creative spirit was at work in the life of Dr. Martin Luther King, Jr., whose vision for non-violent solutions changed a nation. It was at work throughout the life of sculptor Luis Jimenez, author Victor Villaseñor, football star Joe Kapp, and musician Joan Baez. But that same creative spirit also shows up in the adventurous housewife who

transforms limited financial resources into clothing for her family, the inspiring teacher who constantly is able to motivate his students, and low income parents who find a way to send their children to college.

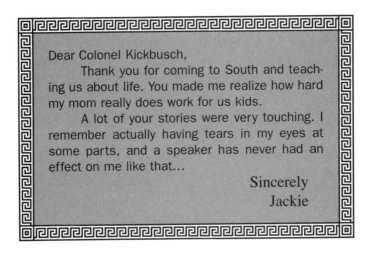

Dear Colonel Kickbusch,

Thank you for coming to South and teaching us about life. You made me realize how hard my mom really does work for us kids.

A lot of your stories were very touching. I remember actually having tears in my eyes at some parts, and a speaker has never had an effect on me like that...

Sincerely
Jackie

Creative people are always thinking about changing something by improving it. They're always tinkering. They're always asking themselves questions like: "What makes sense here? What doesn't look right? How can I improve this? What if I did this to that? What other thing can this be used for? Suppose I combined this with that? What would happen if..."

In addition to the fact that everyone is creative—and that includes you—it is important for you to know that people are generally creative in specific areas. Psychologists refer to these areas as the "seven intelligences. I'm going to mention them here briefly because you are probably gifted in two or more of these areas. That means you can be creative in these areas and make significant contributions to

164

your family, school, church and community. See if you can recognize your "creative niches."

Language: Poets, writers and speakers have a "linguistic intelligence" that sets them apart from other people. They seem to have a way with words. They can create novel combinations of words and phrases that capture different perspectives that are highly innovative.

Math and Logic: This type of intelligence focuses on numerical and computational skills. Mathematicians, scientists, researchers and computer programmers and engineers seem to have this gift. People who are gifted with this type of intelligence can create formulas, computations and logical sequences that astound people who aren't gifted in this way.

Music: People with this gift are attracted to sound in general and music in particular—usually from a young age. They seem to have a perfect ear for music and are quite adept when it comes to working with pitch, resonance and volume.

Spatial Reasoning: This type of intelligence involves the ability to excel in visual (special) relations. People with this gift seem to have a knack for grasping how things work. For example, if you give a young person with this ability a CD player or some other mechanical device, he or she will analyze it, figure out how to take it apart and then reassemble it.

Body Movement: This "genius for movement" as it is called is the ability to use the entire body—through agility, flexibility, strength and stamina—to outperform less gifted competitors. Athletes, dancers, yoga instructors and

extreme sports enthusiasts all have highly developed "body" intelligence.

Interpersonal Savvy: People with this ability are people readers. They have the ability to understand what motivates others and how to work with people in any situation. They have an uncanny ability to influence others by their highly developed persuasive tactics. People who have a gift in this area tend to be the most innovative teachers, ministers, politicians, salespeople, therapists and leaders.

Intrapersonal Savvy: People possessing this type of intelligence know themselves very well. They understand their strengths and weaknesses, abilities and limitations, beliefs and values. They are usually very self-disciplined and decisive. They know how far to push themselves and seem to have an incredible sense of purpose and life direction.

Each one of these intelligences has its own special creative expression and potential. As you read the description of each one of them, you probably identified several that apply to you. I encourage you to develop your "intellectual gift" in one or more of these areas. You could be the next Michael Jordan, Annika Sorenstam, Nancy Lopez, Bill Gates or George Bush. I'm not kidding. Once you develop your special talents and intelligence you can be as creative and successful as you want to be. And you'll be able to do it because you have that special "gift."

All highly creative people seem to have the following things in common:

1. **Creative people believe they are creative**. They recognize how imaginative and innovative they are in certain areas of their lives. They pay attention to small ideas and passing intuitions. Even though it may not be apparent where one of their intuitions will take them, they trust their creative instincts and believe they are capable of coming up with novel ideas.

2. **They look for the second, third, fourth or thirteenth right answer.** Creative people rarely accept the first right answer. They realize that most people jump to conclusions and accept the first quick fix that comes along. Creative people know that when it comes to problem solving, nothing is more dangerous than an idea when it turns out to be the only one you have.

3. **Creative people rarely give blind obedience to rules and assumptions.** The status quo, obsolete rules, tired regulations and ridiculous policies are all red flags to creative people. Although most rules, regulations and policies are necessary and should be honored, there are some that can be changed or even eliminated. Creative people see rules and policies as guides that are there to serve the needs of people, not straight jackets to keep people prisoners.

4. **Creative people have a high tolerance for ambiguity and uncertainty.** They are very comfortable in the midst of change and welcome risks. They enjoy the sense of adventure that comes from meeting newness head on. Creative people rarely like routine and will find creative ways around it.

5. **Creative people ask a lot of questions.** They ask "what if" questions and "why" questions. They ques-

tion everything! They challenge old assumptions. They have a naturally inquisitive nature. They keep their intuitive antennas and their eyes open.

6. **Creative people love to come up with zillions of ideas.** They love to brainstorm for ideas by thinking of as many uses for something or ways of doing something that they can. For example: How many different uses can you think of for a CD? For a drinking straw? For a dime? For a pillow?

7. **Creative people travel off beaten paths.** They explore things they are unfamiliar with and venture into areas where they have little knowledge or expertise. They look for similarities, connections and associations between things in one environment that can be modified, improved and used somewhere else. They know that routine and familiarity cause people to take things for granted and become less aware of their surroundings. Doing something we haven't done before shakes us out of our ruts and helps us gain new perspectives.

8. **Creative people trust their intuition.** Before the Columbine High School shootings in Littleton, Colorado on April 20, 1999, a few students intuitively felt that something tragic was going to happen that day. Several of the students said that their intuition had told them months before the shooting that the widespread teasing they witnessed at school was going to erupt into some kind of violence unless the school administrators took action. Some of those students stayed home that fateful day because their intuitive antennae was so high their "gut instincts" told them to stay home.

Creativity

I am a parent myself. I have five daughters, and I make a living speaking to high schoolers all across America. I wanted to understand why students would want to shoot their classmates in cold blood. Because of my chosen profession I felt I needed to be able to reassure high schoolers, as well as my own daughters that everything would be all right. Both my common sense and intuition told me to prepare myself.

We now know that some of the teenaged shooters blamed their parents, teachers and classmates for not understanding their despondency, humiliation and anger at the classmates who teased them. One of the girls who was shot had had an uneasy feeling about going to school that day, but had decided to go to school anyway.

This is a tragic story about our inability to listen to our intuition, but it reminds us how powerful our intuition can be. On a more positive note, Estee Lauder, founder of the giant cosmetic company which bears her name, was famous for her intuitive ability to pick best selling perfumes. She could out-predict market analysts every time. Linus Pauling, Nobel Prize winner, realized the shape of the protein molecule when he noticed a string of paper dolls resembled the shape of a helix. David Robinson, of the NBA, San Antonio Spurs, used to position himself where he "knew" the rebound would come.

Learn to listen to your "gut feelings," your intuitive nudges. The answers to many of life's questions require more than rational thinking. Sometimes their solutions need "gut guidance" to point us in the right direction. So, liberate your creative spirit and apply it to everything you do, especially when the fates before you do not give you the answers

you need. Adopt creativity as one of your core values so you can get really good at finding creative responses to pressing problems and difficult circumstances.

Remember the story I shared at the beginning of this chapter about Sonya Lopes, the school reform coordinator. She decided that learning should be fun and through her creativity lifted the morale of an entire school in San Mates, California. You can fill your life, and those around you, with "lightness and fun" by expressing your own unique creativity.

Reflection Exercises

1. Release any of your old negative beliefs and attitudes about how uncreative you are by symbolically taking
the following steps:

❖ Write a letter to your negative thoughts, doubts, fears and
concerns about your lack of creative ability. Tell each of
these thoughts what you think about them. Be specific and
to the point. Explain why you no longer want to doubt
your creativity.

❖ Read the letter aloud to yourself.

❖ Now tear up the letter and flush it down the commode.

❖ Promise yourself that from this time forward you will
honor your own creativity.

2. In a notebook, diary or journal, make a list of every single success you've ever experienced in life, as far back
as you can remember. Include successes at home,
school, work, hobbies, volunteer activities, relationships, friendships, travel, health, church and so on.

Read through your list and identify areas you have
experienced more successes in than others. In your
mind's eye, visualize your next meaningful success in
one of those areas. Name two or three of your "upcom-
ing" successes and describe how they will look:

Now, close your eyes again and think about the areas
where you have experienced fewer accomplishments.
Visualize your next meaningful success in one of
those areas. Describe what that success looks like:

3. Pretend you are fifty years older than you are now. Your life story is featured in a prominent magazine. As you read your life story, what are the five most important things, accomplishments, awards, feats or successes you have achieved? List them below. Remember, all of these achievements have taken place over the next fifty years:

4. Answer each of the following ponderables to your own creative satisfaction:

   ❖ How high is up?

   ❖ What color is the wind?

   ❖ Where does your lap go when you stand?

   ❖ What are the sounds of silence?

Every creative act is a liberating
act that lets the spirit sour.

You cannot make yourself feel something you do not feel, but you can make yourself do right in spite of your feelings.   [Pearl S. Buck]

When wealth is lost, nothing is lost; when health is lost, something is lost; when ethics is lost, all is lost.   [Billy Graham]

If people are careless about basic things telling the truth, respecting moral codes, proper conduct   who can believe them on other issues?   [James Hayes]

Chapter 12

Ethics and Morals

*Living ethically and morally
is simple: if it's the right thing
to do—do it!*

During my travels from one school to another around the United States, I have come to realize that there are many decent ethical and moral young people in those schools. So many young people are telling us what they want and what they feel the youth of America need in order to make meaningful contributions. Here is what I hear when I listen to them.

Our young people want, in the words of actress and TV host, Maria Conchita Alonso, "to be respected for what they are inside, for their soul, for the good actions that they do in life, not for how powerful they are or for how much money they have." They want a kinder, gentler world, a place where there is more compassion and love instead of hypocrisy.

They tell me they want less anger and quarreling, an end to fighting, wars and violence. They want a place where people respect each other, share with each other, and help each other. They wish people wouldn't steal from one another or hoard from each other. They believe people shouldn't try to hurt each other or do things to undermine someone's success and happiness.

They want a place where people wouldn't even think of lying to each other; a place that values trust, honesty and fair play; an ethical place where people are treated as equals and judged by the strength of their character and not the color of their skin. Young people want a world where each individual is loved and honored as a human being.

The teens I've spoken with—and listened to—want a chance to develop their talents and skills. They want to be productive citizens, to raise their families in safety, prosperity and peace. They want to live in a nice home and drive a nice car, but they recognize the importance of keeping material things in perspective.

They want their parents to be happy and healthy, whether they are married or divorced. They don't want to be put in the middle of quarreling parents. They want peace, harmony, love and joy at home. Because of their uneasiness about the terrorists' threat, they want their ideas and solutions heard.

They want better schools, safer neighborhoods, ethical CEO's and drug-free homes, neighborhoods and schools.

Our children want stable homes instead of broken homes, student-centered schools and colleges instead of sub-standard educational settings, and school counselors who help them instead of mislead them.

Those are the things young people all across America have told me they want—and one thing more. It's the most important, telling thing of all. I saved it for last because it establishes the basis for the rest of this chapter—and perhaps the theme for this book. It was the item at the top of their list:

> *Young people today want to be able to express who they are and live up to their fullest potential and enjoy all of the freedom they can in an environment where they are nurtured, taught and employed by ethical and moral people.*

Isn't that amazing? The majority of our young people want ethical and moral role models. They want to know right from wrong. One thing is for sure, young people observe their parents, teachers and adults, in general, and make judgments on what they see. Teens are acutely sensitive to inconsistencies between what adults advise and what they do. Actions, as the saying goes, speak louder than words. We shouldn't expect young people to be ethical and moral if all they see is unethical and immoral behavior on the part of adults. Whether it's out of pure rebelliousness, or perhaps simply out of the desire to take responsibility for their actions, young people mimic our hypocrisies. If there is a discrepancy between what is practiced and what is preached by adults, our young people will copy what adults do, not what they preach.

One of my responsibilities as a keynote speaker is to provide young people with a good role model. I try very

hard to do that and take my responsibility seriously. I believe all teachers, counselors and school principals and parents must take their responsibilities seriously, too. And I can't emphasize that enough. Young people have an ethical responsibility, too. We are all human beings and all of us have been empowered with the ability to know right from wrong and to make moral and ethical choices.

I believe there are things each of us can do to keep each other on the right path. I'd like to suggest a few:

- ❖ We can foster a genuine commitment to strengthen our families and help make our homes loving and nurturing places to be.
- ❖ Parents can firmly outline "house rules" along with the underlying justifications of why the rules are important, instead of simply bellowing orders. Young people can see those rules as necessary "guardrails" to protect vital family values and give parents a little credit for wanting to create a nurturing environment.
- ❖ We can show how much we value ethical and moral behavior by acting ethically and morally ourselves.
- ❖ We can participate with each other in social experiences like helping the needy, participating in projects like Habitat for Humanity and Meals on Wheels, taking care of an elderly person's lawn or volunteering for home repairs.
- ❖ We can, by our own ethical and moral actions, let others know we care.
- ❖ We can take the time to engage in hypothetical discussions related to moral and

177

ethical dilemmas so we can learn from each other.

❖ We can speak out against immoral and unethical behavior, instead of giving our silent consent.

❖ We need to recognize someone for acting morally and reinforce that behavior. We can show each other how much we value generosity, truthfulness, unselfishness, kindness, and doing the right thing.

These aren't the only things we can do to reinforce moral and ethical behavior, but they will certainly help us help each other move in the right direction. One thing is for certain, our young people learn from us and they learn from each other. So, it makes sense for them to learn moral and ethical behavior that will make their lives more joyful, happier and productive. The moral and ethical building blocks we help each other forge will determine how susceptible we all become to the pressures and temptations that surround us.

Unfortunately, we are locked in a constant moral battle with a continually arrogant media that forces alluring advertising, silly TV programming, obscene music, sexually explicit commercials, substance abuse, despicable reality shows and absurd talk shows on us. I make no apologies when I say that, in addition to my focus on educating our young people to stay in school, I am doing everything my time and talents allow to blunt the unethical intentions of media empires that prize money and material possessions above decency and morality. I believe I am fighting for the souls of our children. And, thankfully, I am not alone.

It has been my experience that both adults and young people must move morality and ethics from theory to practice. One of our goals as teachers, coaches, scout leaders,

clergymen, principals—and keynote speakers—is to help young people make ethical and moral decisions when we are not around. They must be able to self-monitor their own behavior and intentions. By involving them in discussions about moral dilemmas, both real and fictitious, they will be able to learn how to handle themselves in situations that test their character. Ethical and moral behavior will become ingrained so they can instinctively make the right choices.

The author and former Catholic monk, Thomas Moore, pointed out: "Nurturing the soul does not mean telling people *the* right path to clarity and success. It's more about helping them sort out the issues involved." He makes an excellent point. It has been my experience when young people are spoon-fed rigid moral rules or lessons, one of two things happens—they accept the rules at face value or rebel against them.

Even if we have clear moral intentions and understand right from wrong, our clarity and obedience to those principles can become compromised if we're not careful. Our commitment to our morals depends on our circumstances and sometimes those circumstances prompt us to do things we ordinarily wouldn't do. Put yourself in each of the following ethical dilemmas. Come to terms with each of the scenarios in your own mind first, then ask a friend, parent, teacher, coach, scout leader or clergyman for his or her input:

The most popular person in your class asks you to write his/her school report. He/she offers some kind of excuse to justify why he/she can't do the assignment and tells you how much he/she admires your writing

ability. You've always wanted to get close to this person and see his/her request as a way to become one of the "in crowd." What would you do, and why would you do it?

You are at a party and your friends are drinking beer and taking drugs. You don't like the taste of beer and have never taken drugs. One of your friends entices you to take a drink, just one sip. Another approaches you and asks if you've ever tried Ecstasy. Several of your friends insist you try both as a way of "coming of age," or "joining the real party." Everyone seems to be having a good time and you feel a little awkward being the only one who has abstained from alcohol and drug use. Your closest friend tries both and urges you to do the same. What would you do? Why would you do it?

As you can see our commitment to our morals can be very difficult at times. So often it depends on the situation we find ourselves in unless we have really matured in our moral and ethical outlooks. Here are five questions you can ask yourself whenever you are faced with a moral dilemma. They will help you decide right from wrong:

1. Will what I am about to do hurt anyone?
2. Does what I intend to do have any negative or destructive consequences?
3. Is what I am about to do illegal, unethical or immoral?

4. Would I be ashamed or embarrassed to tell anyone about it?

5. If I were to get caught doing it, would I consider what I did to be right or wrong?

The first question is based on the Golden Rule: Do unto others are you would have them do unto you. It asks you to ask yourself, "Would I like it if someone did it to me?" The second question asks us to consider the consequences of our decision: its physical, mental, emotional, financial and spiritual implications. It is easy to see why drug abuse and alcohol are wrong because of their disastrous unhealthy effects. Promiscuous sex can have its ill effects, too, in the form of STD's (sexually transmitted diseases). Having a baby implies a host of responsibilities, the least of which include: clothing, sheltering, feeding, educating, loving, protecting and providing health care.

The third question involves obeying the law and abiding by the moral and ethical standards established by the society in which you live. Sometimes it means having higher standards than those practiced by society. The fourth question involves your own conscience. Will you think highly of yourself or lose a little self-respect? Will you do what is right or sell your soul? The fifth question involves willfully and knowing violating your set of moral or ethical beliefs, getting caught and suffering the humiliation associated with letting important people down—including yourself.

I believe that if you apply all five of those questions to any moral or ethical dilemma, you will do the right thing. There are no absolute formulas for moral success, but I believe these questions come close. I also believe we are all pre-wired for moral and ethical behavior. If we listen to that

"still, small voice" which comes from within us, we can be moral and ethical people.

> Dear Colonel Kickbusch,
>
> I wanna tell you that your speech was amazing. You sure know how to speak to an audience. I wish I could do that. The part that touched me the most, was the part about treating our moms the way they deserve to be treated. I would be devastated if anything happened to my mom. Because of your speech I learned that I should talk to my mom everyday, ask her how she's feeling, and ask her if I can help her in any way. And not just my mom, my dad, too. They are the best parents ever. Your speech was the most wonderful speech I've ever heard in my short life. I hope that sometime you will come back again and share more experiences with us. I surely hope you will come back. I'm Hispanic, too, and know how it feels to be rejected.
>
> Thank you very much for coming, and we will be waiting to see you again.
>
> Sincerely,
> Mirna

Reflection Exercises

1. One of the simplest ways to know what is right and what is wrong is to chose words that describe what you are about to do. I have composed a set of words to help you make better choices. If what you are about to do can be described using the words on the left, it's probably the right thing to do. If it is characterized by the words on the right, it's something you probably should refrain from doing:

Words Which Characterize Right Actions	Words Which Characterize Unethical or Self-Defeating Actions
Accountable, responsible	Irresponsible, untrustworthy
Appreciative, thankful	Ungrateful, discourteous
Benevolent, charitable	Selfish, miserly
Caring, considerate, courteous	Inconsiderate, neglectful
Compassionate, loving	Harsh, merciless, hateful
Courageous, brave, valiant	Cowardly, fearful
Determined, committed	Indecisive, unfocused
Disciplined, dedicated	Unfocused, irresponsible
Enthusiastic, energetic, cheerful	Bored, dull, tired
Faithful, loyal	Disloyal, traitor
Forgiving, merciful	Vengeful, spiteful, ruthless
Generous, giving, kind	Greedy, stingy, hoarding, rude
Gentle, calm	Cruel, harsh, oppressive
Honest, trustworthy, integrity	Cheater, liar, corrupt
Honorable	Despicable, disgraceful
Hopeful, patient	Impatient
Humble	Arrogant, conceited, egotistical
Joyful, happy	Gloomy, unhappy, depressed
Learned, educated	Illiterate, uneducated
Mature, adult-like	Immature, naive
Open-minded	Biased, close-minded
Patriotic, public-spirited	Traitor, turncoat, conspirator
Peaceful, law-abiding	Violent, disruptive, caustic
Respectful, considerate	Disrespectful, insolent insulting
Trustworthy, reliable	Doubtful, suspicious
Understanding, insightful, aware	Intolerant, biased, prejudicial

2. Think of a situation in which you can apply the following two words: *Forgiveness* and *compassion*. It could be an issue you are currently facing, a past issue or a future concern. See yourself, in your mind's eye, approaching it from the standpoint of *forgiveness* and *compassion*. When you think you are ready, show that person how forgiving and compassionate you can be. Once you've acted on these two words, pick two more positive words and follow the same process: visualize the successful outcome, have faith that doing the right thing will bring you positive results, and then take action.

Reflect on the differences between these two sets of words. They will help steer you in the right direction. If you think about your actions ahead of time and do the right thing to begin with, you will dramatically increase your chances of benefiting from a positive outcome.

3. Ethical behavior is based on personal integrity and trust. It is important to be consistent in your behaviors, communicate clearly and honestly, keep realistic promises, protect confidences and treat others with respect. It takes time to build this type of reputation; it is a process that makes each step very important. The following exercises will help you think about your ethics and help you plan your next steps.

Do your family, friends and teachers (employers) view you as a person of ethical behavior? Answer the following questions to determine your level of ethics:

* Do you consistently make realistic promises and keep them?

* When you are questioned or challenged, do you give honest answers?

* Do you admit your mistakes?

* Do you consider the trust and confidence of your family, friends and teachers as important?

* Do you make an effort to communicate in an open, honest and sincere manner?

* Do you encourage others to question things with which they disagree?

* Do you follow the rules of your home, school or employer as a guide for making ethical decisions?

* Do your words and actions match?

* Do you listen to others and give them time to ask questions?

4. The questions you just answered are reminders of what ethical behavior looks like. A "yes" answer indicates that you are able to establish and maintain open and trusting relationships. Go back over the questions again and give an example of how you made an ethical choice in the past for each question.

5. Making ethical decisions can be broken down into several manageable steps. Place a check mark next to each step that you take when you are faced with an ethical dilemma:

❑ I ask myself, "What is the issue?"

❑ I think about the importance of any consequences in the short term.

❑ I think about the importance of any consequences in the long term.

❑ I consider if there might be anything keeping me from seeing the whole situation.

❑ How would I advise someone else if they came to me with this same dilemma?

❑ Is the situation harmful or dangerous to anyone?

❑ A year from now, will I be proud of myself for the decision I need to make now?

❑ What would my parents or teachers do?

❑ Would I be proud if my decision were published in the newspaper or broadcast on my favorite TV or radio station?

- ❏ If I don't know what to do, am I willing to ask for help from someone in a leadership position?

- ❏ Is the dilemma about something that is illegal?

6. Who are some of your role models when it comes to ethical behavior? Use the chart below to think about who they are and why you selected them for this question:

<u>Behavior</u>   <u>Name of Person</u>

This person makes realistic promises and keeps them . . . .

This person faces up to challenges with honest answers. . . . .

This person keeps confidential or sensitive information to herself/himself. . . . .

This person admits when he/she has made a mistake. . . . .

This person is open, honest and sincere in his/her communications. . . . .

This person is not afraid to question things with which he/she disagrees. . . . .

This person follows the rules to make ethical decisions. . . . .

This person does what she/he says they are going to do. . . . .

This person listens, and gives others time to ask questions. . . . .

3. Think of an important moral or ethical dilemma you have facing you. Review the five questions on page 180. Ask yourself all five of these questions before you make your decision. Promise yourself you will adapt this strategy whenever you are faced with a moral dilemma.

In almost every situation imaginable, matters of right and wrong are obvious.

Faith becomes a tool for taking further risks, and these risks generate further faith, which generates the possibility of further risk.

[Julia Cameron]

Faith is the continuation of reason.

[William James]

You block your dreams when you allow your fear to grow bigger than your faith.

[Mary Manin Morrissey]

Chapter 13

Faith in Positive Outcomes

With faith, all things are possible.

It is my fervent prayer that millions of young people's lives will be transformed by influential and responsible adult role models as parents, teachers, school counselors and coaches take a more active role in helping our nation's young people experience what it means to be loved and appreciated. As we raise our children—from diapers to diplomas—there is one overarching responsibility that all adults have in common: the moral and educational growth of our children.

One such child received the moral education she needed, and her faith and moral witness will forever be etched in the collective memory of people all over America and the world. A horrible tragedy took place in America on April 20, 1999. I mentioned the Columbine High School shootings in Chap-

ter 11 from the perspective of listening to our intuition. I recount it here from the standpoint of faith and courage.

Twelve wonderful young people and one courageous teacher lost their lives that day. One of those students was a bright seventeen-year-old girl named Rachel Scott. She, like dozens of others, was taunted and questioned about her faith at gunpoint. Her attackers, two misguided, angry young boys, demanded that she stop praying. She calmly refused. They aimed their guns at her and fired. Her last words were a confirmation of the faith she lived and her death was a testimony to her unfaltering courage as she forgave her murderers.

There have been shootings in other schools since the tragic events at Columbine. Since the dawn of creation there have been both good and evil in the hearts of men, women, boys and girls. We all contain the seeds of loving kindness or kernels of violence. It is this realization that prompted me to include this chapter in this book. I believe faith and morality must become two of the core values in our homes, schools, communities, businesses and nation if we really want America to live up to her promise.

So, what holds us together? What keeps us from falling off the deep end?

The remarkable ecologist, Machaelle Wright Smith, whose farm Perelandra has been called an American Findhorn, explains how she sees the moral and ethical threads work. (The Findhorn is the famous Scottish garden where an incredible number of varieties of flora flourish on barren soil.) In her book, she writes:

I can't adequately express how wholeheartedly I recommend the search for…(moral and ethical) threads…in every life experience…By seeking (these) threads I see the purpose contained within individual events and how each event is built on top of the previous ones, creating a pattern of wholeness. I can see the light of synthesis. The result has been that more and more I don't look back in anger and disappointment. Instead, I look forward in faith and celebration.

Her "pattern of wholeness" description reminds me of those clever pictures and puzzles that at first glance look like photographs of someone, but upon closer inspection are in fact composed of hundreds of little pictures. All of the little pictures make up the big picture. I'm sure you've seen them. At a distance the pictures "thread themselves" into a pattern of wholeness that can't be seen up close.

Imagine looking at a very large picture of yourself that, as you look more closely, is made up of thousands of smaller pictures of all the significant moments of your life. From the time you were born until now, every experience of your life is represented: birthdays, holidays, school days, work experiences, awards and achievements, quiet moments and party moments, times when sickness slowed you down, dating experiences, etc. There are even pictures that captured those moments when you thought no one was looking. All of those snapshots combine to make up the big picture of who you are today.

How many of those pictures are higher-calling snapshots? How many depict times when you connected with your inner peace? Which ones show your selfless qualities? Are there any which show you on your knees in gratefulness? Do you have a religious text in your hand in any of the pictures?

Dear Mrs. Kickbusch,

Today you spoke to the students at South High, and it was touching. Many students who would think of themselves as the victims started thinking about their parents and how they were really receiving more than they deserved. You let them know of the events that can happen from the decisions and that they should make their choices more carefully without having peer pressure influence them. Your manner of speaking was also very effective to reach into the students, you used examples that they could easily identify and relate to, without having to ask other people. I thank you for your time. I know that being a CEO of a corporation requires much of your time, thank you once again for coming.

Sincerely,

Hipolito

The good news is that we only need to concentrate on one picture at a time. Each little picture—each life experience—is up to us. We can make it a happy one or a sad one, a loving one or a hateful one, a calm one or emotional one, a drug-filled one or a courage-filled one. It's up to us! Each decision, every choice, every direction we take colors our big picture. Our portrait can be shaded with self-interest, deceit, anger and violence or brightened with kindness, self-discipline, honesty, compassion, respect and faith.

How can we make our big picture one of wholeness, strength, success, peace and joy? I sincerely believe 99 percent of it comes from good choices and 1 percent (a mustard seed) from faith. All of us—parents, teachers, coaches, counselors, school administrators and students—need to give each other three very important things when it comes to strengthening our character: an unshakable faith, an internal compass and an unwavering example of big picture wholeness. Let's look at each of these.

An Unshakable Faith

Artist Amalia Mesa-Bains shared the story about surviving an often fatal pulmonary illness in Yoland Nava's book, *It's All in the Frijoles:*

I became very, very seriously ill with an illness which is usually fatal. I'm very sure that my mother's prayers and the prayers of others, along with the changes I've made in my life, account for the return of my health.

Throughout my life, I've been tested several times over the issue of faith and my religion. I've come to realize that it is…the belief in a higher power that makes the difference. Many people struggle with challenges far greater than mine. I believe their unshakable faith makes them strong, resilient and capable of living through really difficult situations.

Luis Valdez, the director and founder of *El Teatro Campesino* shares a similar belief in the power of unshakable faith:

> *I learned from my mother that (faith) is not just a tool for a crisis, but a daily way of living...She was always telling people to be wary of 'los elementos negativos,' negative elements, (like) doubt, self-hatred and anything else that prevents us from having an unshakable faith.*

> *One of the greatest lessons I learned from my mother was that only (a strong character) can get you where you want to go in life. The path you choose is not important because all paths lead to your future. These are two key lessons my mother taught me, legacies of her unshakable faith.*

We need to have faith in ourselves—to believe in ourselves. But before we can believe in ourselves, we must have faith that comes from outside of ourselves—faith in a higher being. For me, my inner peace comes from my strong faith. In my darkest moments, I know there will be answers. Sometimes, I am provided with answers that have not been clear to me until weeks, months and even years later! However, I know that the answers provided have not been hurtful to me. Those answers have strengthened and supported me. And I believe that if you will listen for the answers, you will receive them—maybe not in the way you expect, but they will always come in the way you need.

An Internal Compass

I'd like you to help me out with a little experiment. Close your eyes and sit comfortably where you are. Now, with your eyes still closed, point in the direction of *true north*. Keep pointing and open your eyes. Are you sure you are pointing to *true north?* How could you be sure? One of the best ways to find *true north* is by using a compass. It would be interesting to see how close you were when you pointed to what you thought was *true north* if you had a compass nearby.

I used this example to make an important point: Your inner wisdom is your *True North*. It doesn't matter how turned around we are or how confused we become in the midst of our every day pressures and concerns. If we take a few moments to center ourselves and find our *True North,* we will be able to find our way out of any circumstance or difficulty.

Our inner guidance is our internal compass. It uses our conscience and intuition to guide us toward *True North*. If we trust our inner instincts anytime we need to make important decisions, I believe we will always get the right answers.

In order to achieve the success you want, you must find appropriate role models and spend time with them, if possible. Certain people up-lift us, others seem to pull us down. Certain people give us strength and energy, others drain our energy. Choosing the right role models is essential to our success, and I believe part of this "rightness" is choosing role models who are grounded in virtues such as honesty, compassion, humility, self-discipline and integrity. They also should have a strong work ethic and have creativity as one of their core values.

Role models who have these qualities are more numerous than you might think, but you've got to find them. You can tell who they are by examining their attitudes, actions, achievements, and by the "company" they keep. True role

models will be just that—role models. They will not deviate from their principles or compromise their integrity. They will come across your "radar" screen as genuine and authentic. Your own sense of *True North* will lead you to them.

Finding "big picture of wholeness" role models may sound like a tall order until we remember that each small step, every leap of faith comes one experience at a time. I firmly believe that if you adopt each of the core values outlined in this book your leaps of faith will be grounded on solid principles. I have experienced this many times in my own life and want you to always remember: with faith, all things are possible—and everything works together for good.

Reflection Exercises

1. Use any resources available to you, such as books, responsible adults, the library, your own ideas, etc to define "inner guidance."

2. Use any resources available to you to define "Faith."

3. What are your religious beliefs?

4. Describe your level of faith.

5. Remember the exercises in the chapter on Identity? You were asked to name some people you admire. Look back at that list. What do those people whom you admire believe in? Do they believe in something or someone, a higher being who guides their lives? List their names on the following chart and describe their courage and faith.

Person I Admire	COURAGE	FAITH

6. Imagine it is 60–70 years from today. People are sitting at a coffee shop talking about you and how you were when you were much younger. What will they be saying about you, your courage and your faith?

7. Under what circumstances is it hard for you to find True North? Describe your dilemma.

8. If you had unwavering faith in your ability to take an ethical, moral stand, what you do?

Sing, hum, laugh your wandering soul back "Home."

We hold these truths to be self-evident, that all [people] are created equal; that they are endowed by their Creator with certain unalienable rights, that among these are life, liberty and the pursuit of happiness.

[The Declaration of Independence]

I have a dream   children will one day live in a nation where they will not be judged by the color of their skin but by the content of their character.   [Dr. Martin Luther King, Jr.]

Since this country was founded, each generation of Americans has been summoned to give testimony to its national loyalty.

[John F. Kennedy]

Chapter 14

Duty, Honor, Country

Duty to our country is the
currency of patriotism.

I f love for one's country is not a core value, I don't know what is. I would like to think that in our collective hearts as U.S. citizens, we share the conviction that every human being has the right to "life, liberty and the pursuit of happiness"– and that no mere mortal has the right to take from another mortal this precious gift of liberty.

The true mark of a great nation is its ability to withstand and benefit from a noisy and independent citizenry that has its own opinions about freedom, responsibility, rights and privileges. I believe one of the litmus tests of America will be its ability to educate its young people with enough passion, love, competence and judgment to under-

stand that everyone in this wonderfully diverse nation bears the ultimate responsibility for America's success or failure.

It is with this responsibility in mind that I decided to include a chapter on duty, honor and country. It is my sincere hope that all of the young people who read this book, and this chapter in particular, will value the richness of America and strive to add their unique contributions so that America can live up to her promise to provide life, liberty and happiness for all of its people.

It is also my great desire that all of the adults who read this book, and this chapter in particular, will accept their responsibility to ensure that educational, family, work and church environments nurture our young people's growth and development and dignify the sacrifices of so many of our armed service veterans who have given their lives for America and the freedom America represents. We are free because so many of our sons and daughters have paid the ultimate price for our freedom, both domestically and abroad.

It is with a great deal of pride that I served in the U.S. Army for 20 years. Eight out of ten of my brothers and sisters also served in the armed forces. When I retired as a Lieutenant Colonel, I "enlisted" in a career that has become my life's work. I accepted the "tour of duty" in order to honor the wishes of my dying mother, who saw my next command as more ministerial than military. I guess you could say I'm a recruiter of sorts. I recruit young people all across America to stay in school and to stay focused on becoming happy, healthy, prosperous adults.

I feel both blessed — and driven—to fulfill those responsibilities. I feel a sense of duty to young people across America who are struggling, confused, hurt and angry. I feel a keen sense of obligation to help parents, teachers and community leaders provide healthy social

environments for young people, because it takes a community to raise a child. I am also duty-bound to uphold the high standards of citizenship and loyalty I learned in the Army and apply those standards to my civilian life and professional career to improve America— one student at a time.

Dear Colonel Kickbusch,

All of us at Omaha South High School, staff and students, would like to thank you for coming to speak to us. I loved your presentation, which focused on being successful, being a leader and respecting yourself and everyone else. You are a very successful Hispanic woman and overall person. This makes you highly respected and looked up on, and I think the speech showed this a lot. The whole presentation was very touching, but the part about us all being Americans, no matter what your race, age, or origin.

everyone in the U.S. is American. I think everyone should support and take pride in being this. Not enough people are re joining our armed forces and that is sad. We should all protect the United States of America and its great freedom.

Sincerely,

Spencer

I can think of no better way to present a chapter on duty, honor and country than to share excerpts from great Americans and great American documents. They are ones I believe every American should read from time to time. I read them to rekindle the American spirit within me—and to honor those brave Americans, past, present and future, who have contributed, and will contribute, to America's greatness.

I hope you will read the following patriotic excerpts with interest and reverence. Their themes will speak to the student you, the teacher you, the school counselor you, the parent you, the coach you, the administrator you, the clergyman you, the business person you. They will speak to the young you, the old you, the single parent you, the divorced you, the married you, the unemployed you, the over-worked you—the American you.

The first entry is an excerpt from an immortal declaration. The Declaration of Independence stands as one of the truly heroic documents of recorded history. In one sudden sweep, humankind vaulted to an entirely new level of political life, and a new kind of freedom. What had been only a matter of philosophical debate had become a political reality. Perhaps more than any other single document, the Declaration represents a watershed in human history–because for the first time in recorded history, our Founders brought the concepts of freedom, liberty and equality into legal, moral and emotional reality:

Declaration of Independence
(excerpt)

We hold these truths to be self-evident, that all men are created equal, that they are endowed by their Creator with certain unalienable rights, that among these are life, liberty and the pursuit of happiness. That to secure these rights, governments are instituted among men, deriving their just powers from the consent of the governed ... laying its foundation on such principles and organizing its powers in such form, as to them shall seem most likely to effect their safety and happiness. And for the support of this declaration, with a firm reliance on the protection of Divine Providence, we mutually pledge to each other our lives, our fortunes, and our sacred honor.

Patrick Henry's Famous "Give Me Liberty" Speech
March of 1775
(excerpt)

It is only in this way that we can hope to arrive at truth, and fulfill the great responsibility which we hold to ... our country ... If we wish to be free; if we mean to preserve inviolate those inestimable privileges for which we have been so long contending ... we must fight!

Millions of people armed in the holy cause of liberty, and in such a country as that which we possess, are invincible by any force which our enemy can send against us.

Is life so dear, or peace so sweet, as to be purchased at the price of chains and slavery? Forbid it! I know not what course others may take, but as for me, give me liberty, or give me death!

Lincoln's Gettysburg Address

No American reading the Gettysburg Address can miss Lincoln's message—his emphasis was on continuity, challenge, sacrifice and devotion. By acknowledging the supremacy of what the soldiers did, he touched the very essence of duty, honor and country. And he saw the outcome of the battle as no golden victory, but as an opportunity, purchased at great human cost, for the living to resolve to do their part to continue to keep the experiment in free government alive.

For those of you who want to keep the experiment in free government alive for your children and your grandchildren; and for their children and grandchildren and for those who have given their lives for freedom, I encourage you to take Abraham Lincoln's Gettysburg Address to heart:

Fourscore and seven years ago our fathers brought forth on this continent a new nation, conceived in liberty, and dedicated to the proposition that all men are created equal.

Now we are engaged in a great civil war, testing whether that nation, or any nation so conceived and so dedicated, can long endure. We are met on a great battlefield of that war. We have come to dedicate a portion of that field as a final resting-place for those who here gave their lives that that nation might live. It is altogether fitting and proper that we should do this.

But, in a larger sense, we cannot dedicate—we cannot consecrate—we cannot hallow—this ground. The brave men, living and dead, who struggled here, have consecrated it far above our poor power to add or detract. The world will little note nor long remember what we say here, but it can never forget what they did here. It is for us, the living, rather, to be dedicated here to the unfinished work which they who fought here have thus far so nobly advanced. It is rather for us to be here dedicated to the great task remaining before us—that from these honored dead we take increased devotion to that cause for which they gave the last full measure of devotion; that we here highly

resolve that these dead shall not have died in vain'
that this nation ... shall have a new birth of freedom;
and that government of the people, by the people, for
the people, shall not perish from the earth.

President Franklin Delano Roosevelt's "Human Freedom" Speech
(excerpt)

In the future days which we seek to make secure, we
look forward to a world founded upon four essential
human freedoms:

The first is freedom of speech and expression–every-
where in the world.

The second is freedom of every person to worship ...
in his own way–everywhere in the world.

The third is freedom from want. ...

The fourth is freedom from fear. ...

This great Nation will endure ... revive and prosper.
... Let me assert my firm belief that the only thing we
have to fear is fear itself–nameless, unreasoning,
unjustified terror which paralyzes needed efforts to
covert retreat into advance. In every dark hour of our
national life a leadership of frankness and vigor has
met with that understanding and support of the peo-
ple themselves which is essential to victory.

Journey to the Future

President Woodrow Wilson's "Genesis of America" Speech
(excerpt)

When I look back on the processes of history, when I survey the genesis of America, I see this written over every page: that nations are renewed from the bottom, not from the top; that the genius which springs up from the ranks of the (people) is the genius which renews the youth and energy of the people. Everything I know about history...has confirmed...the conviction that the real wisdom of human life is compounded out of the experiences of ordinary (people).

President John F. Kennedy's 1961 Inaugural Address
(excerpt)

We dare not forget today that we are the heirs of that first revolution. Let the word go forth from this time and place, to friend and foe alike, that the torch has been passed to a new generation of Americans–born in this century, tempered by war, disciplined by a hard and bitter peace, proud of our ancient heritage–and unwilling to witness or permit the slow undoing of those human rights to which this Nation has always been committed ...

Let us begin anew–remembering that civility is not a sign of weakness, and sincerity is always subject to proof. Let us never negotiate out of fear. But let us never fear to negotiate.

Let us explore what problems unite us instead of laboring those problems which divide us. ...

In your hands, my fellow citizens, more than in mine, will rest the final success or failure of our course. Since this country was founded, each generation of Americans has been summoned to give testimony to its national loyalty. ...

And so, my fellow Americans, ask not what your country can do for you; ask what you can do for your country.

Dr. Martin Luther King, Jr.'s "I Have a Dream" Speech (excerpt)

Five score years ago, a great American, in whose symbolic shadow we stand today, signed the Emancipation Proclamation. This momentous decree came as a great beacon light of hope to millions of (our ancestors) who had been seared in the flames of withering injustice. ...

We have also come to this hallowed spot to remind America (that) this is no time to engage in the luxury of cooling off or to take the tranquilizing drug of gradualism. Now is the time to make real the promises of democracy; ... now is the time to make justice a reality for all ... children. ...

I have a dream my four little children will one day live in a nation where they will not be judged by the color of their skin but by the content of their character. ...

I have a dream that one day every valley shall be exalted, every hill and mountain shall be made low, the rough places shall be made plain, and the crooked places shall be made straight and the glory of the Lord will be revealed …

With this faith we will be able to work together, to pray together, to struggle together, to stand up for freedom together …

It is my sincere hope that you took the time to read—and perhaps reread—these truly great excerpts from extraordinary Americans. My goal was to create a sense of pride, reverence—and urgency—within you to renew your commitment to making America a better home for all of us. Join me in honoring America and your place in it so our voices are not merely those of a soloist, but a choir.

One such soloist, Todd Beamer, courageously rushed the cockpit in United Flight 93 before terrorists could use the plane as a bomb to kill Americans. He speaks for all of us whenever someone threatens our life, liberty and freedom. In honor of his last words, if we ever find ourselves facing threats to our freedom, individuality, dignity and self-respect—"Let's Roll" to the tune of The Star Spangled Banner, our national anthem and the wisdom of the Golden Rule.

Reflection Exercises

1. Find a copy of *The Book of Great American Documents* in your local library or your school library, and read the following documents in their entirety. They will stir your soul:

- ❖ The Declaration of Independence, 1776
- ❖ The Bill of Rights, 1791
- ❖ The Emancipation Proclamation, 1863
- ❖ The Gettysburg Address, 1863
- ❖ Kennedy's Inaugural Address, 1961

Also find a copy of Dr. Martin Luther King's inspiring "I Have a Dream" speech. Revisit each of these "duty, honor, country" documents periodically. They will deepen your appreciation for what America stands for and why all of us must become better citizens—no matter how long we have been a citizen.

2. Listed below are several "duty, honor, country" activities that characterize people who love and value what America stands for. Check all of the activities that you have accomplished which show your loyalty to the American Spirit:

❒ I have read each of the great American documents listed in Exercise One in their entirety.

❒ I support War Veterans in a number of ways.

❒ I vote responsibly in political elections.

❒ I do volunteer work in my community.

- ☐ I do not trash our environment (waterways, highways, parks, city streets, etc.)
- ☐ I know the words to *The Star Spangled Banner* and *America the Beautiful*.
- ☐ I go to 4th of July and Veterans Day parades and festivals.
- ☐ I have visited the Vietnam War Memorial, Korean War Memorial and War Nurses Memorial in Washington D.C.
- ☐ I display the American Flag on Flag Day, June 14th.
- ☐ I visit historical sites and battlefields whenever I can to get a sense for the sacrifices others have made to ensure my freedom.
- ☐ I write or email Congressional leaders and voice my opinion on important American issues.
- ☐ I crusade against drugs and alcohol, drunk driving, school violence, teenage pregnancies, corrupt government officials, child abuse and spousal abuse whenever I can.

3. In the space provided below, explain what you can do right now to be a shining example of someone who takes "duty, honor and country" seriously.

Listen to the conscientious voice of duty.

Your Thoughts & Feedback

I would enjoy hearing your thoughts, your suggestions, your concerns—in short, anything that you may want to share regarding this book and what it has meant to you. You will find my contact information at my website: www.latinaspeaker.com

If you would like Consuelo to come to your school, talk to your counselors and administrators to see if this can be arranged. They may contact us at our toll free number:
(888) 354-4747

Service or information inquiries:
admin@latinaspeaker.com
Product sales: admin@latinaspeaker.com

Pledge to Yourself

Many times it is easier to promise to someone else what you think you can deliver than to promise it to yourself. I have included this Pledge to Yourself so that you may make the promise to yourself that you will take action on some of the materials in this booklet.

Use the space below to record the actions you pledge to yourself you will take. Be sure to sign this pledge at the bottom—that makes it a legal document to yourself!

As a result of reading Journey to the Future, I pledge to take the following actions to create my roadmap to success:

_____

Signature and Date

Bibliography

American History Research Assoc., *The Book of Great American Documents*, Crawfordsville, Ind.: RR Donnelley & Sons, 1993.

Blaisdell, Etta Austin & Mary Frances Blaisdell, "Little Sunshine," as quoted in *Ghost Stories,* Raleigh, NC: Liberty Publishing Group, 2003.

Breathnach, Sarah Ban, *Simple Abundance: A Daybook of Comfort and Joy,* New York: Warner Books, 1995.

Coyote Chuck Jones as quoted in *The Creative Spirit* by Daniel Goldman, Paul Kaufman and Michael Ray, New York: Dutten Books, 1992.

Dyer, Wayne, *Wisdom of the Ages,* New York: Harper Collins, 1998.

Haney, William, *Communication and Interpersonal Relations,* Homewood, ILL.: Richard Irwin, 1979.

Kopp, Sheldon, *Rock, Paper, Scissors,* CompCare Publishers, Minneapolis, Minn., 1985.

Loomis, Earl, "The Self in Pilgrimage," as quoted in *Umpteen Amazing Quotes,* Raleigh, NC: Liberty Publishing Group, 2003.

McGraw, Jay, *Daily Life Strategies for Teens,* New York: Simon and Schuster, March 19, 2002.

Nava, Yoland, *It's all in the Frijoles,* New York: Fireside, 2000.

Nearing, Helen, *Loving and Leaving the Good Life,* South Burlington, VT: Chelsea Green, 2003.

Quinn, Anthony, *One Man Tango,* New York: HarperCollins Pub., 1995.

Smith, Machaelle Wright, *Behaving As If the God in All Life Matters,* Warrenton, VA: Perelandra, Ltm., 1987.

Sonya Lopes as quoted in Kouzes, James and Barry Posner, *Encouraging the Heart,* San Francisco, CA: Jossey-Bass, 1999.

Teresa, Mother, *Mother Teresa: In My Own Words,* compiled by José Luis Gonzales—Balado, New York: Random House, 1996.

Underhill, Daryl Ott, *Every Woman Has a Story,* New York: Warner Books, 1999.

Williams, Terrie, *Stay Strong: Simple Life Lessons for Teens,* New York: Scholastic Inc. 2001.

215

Index

E

F

G

H

I

J

K

About the Author

Born and raised in a tiny barrio in Laredo, Texas, where she overcame the fierce challenges of poverty, discrimination and illiteracy, **Consuelo Castillo Kickbusch** grew to become a successful leadership role model for her community. Breaking barriers and setting records in the military, she rose to the position of Lieutenant Colonel, becoming the highest-ranking Hispanic woman in the Combat Support Field of the United States Army. Acknowledged as a charismatic, passionate and entertaining speaker, Consuelo carries her powerful message of what it takes to be an effective leader in today's global marketplace to hundreds of colleges/ universities, corporations and government institutions, both in the U.S. and abroad.

Her strong dedication to saving the youth of America, especially those living in the same barrios she did as a child, has led Consuelo into some of the roughest neighborhoods in America, where she has worked with over one million children, parents and educators covering 43 states. She inspires these young "diamonds in the rough" to believe they can make their dreams come true, and encourages them to never give up hope, but rather take responsibility to make a real difference in their families/communities and follow a disciplined road map to success.

The *Hispanic Business Magazine* recently included Consuelo Kickbusch, Lt. Col., U.S. Army (ret) as one of the 100 Most Influential Hispanics in America.